THE WRITING PROCESS

THE
WRITING
PROCESS

Richard Davey
Sheridan College

Prentice-Hall Canada Inc., Scarborough, Ontario

Canadian Cataloguing in Publication Data

Davey, Richard, 1949—
    The writing process

Includes index.
ISBN 0-13-972001-4

1. Exposition (Rhetoric). 2. English language—
Rhetoric. 3. Report writing. I. Title.

LB2369.D38 1984   808'.042   C83-099100-X

Prentice-Hall, Inc., Englewood Cliffs, New Jersey
Prentice-Hall International, Inc., London
Prentice-Hall of Australia, Pty., Ltd., Sydney
Prentice-Hall of India Pvt., Ltd., New Delhi
Prentice-Hall of Japan, Inc., Tokyo
Prentice-Hall of Southeast Asia (Pte.) Ltd., Singapore
Editora Prentice-Hall do Brasil Ltda., Rio de Janeiro

ISBN 0-13-972001-4

Production Editors: Rebecca Vogan, Neil Gallaiford
Design: Pat Gangnon
Production: Monika Heike
Typesetting: Fleet Typographers

Printed and bound in Canada by Webcom Limited
1   2   3   4   5   WC   88   87   86   85   84

Contents

RE-WRITING 81

Introduction

Writing is a craft. Like ceramics, dress-making or building model airplanes, writing has a starting point and a specific process. To the accomplished, there is nothing mysterious about this step-by-step approach. At each step, the craftsperson makes decisions and uses developed skills. This book shows you how to work through a writing process. It presents the decisions and teaches the skills necessary to write effective college and career-related projects.

The writing process has three stages: **pre-writing, writing** and **re-writing**. Chapters 1 to 6 examine the **pre-writing** stage. In this part of the process, you define the writing problem and begin to wrestle with what you want to say. During pre-writing, you work to find the best material, to control that material and to organize your writing.

The **writing** stage of the process is presented in Chapters 7 and 8. When you write your first draft, you are turning a pre-writing plan into sentences and paragraphs. Writing a first draft requires some decisions about word usage and style. Reviewing that draft calls for some knowledge of structure and some hard questions about the effectiveness of the draft.

In Chapters 9 through 14 you'll learn what to examine and how to re-write your draft sentences. **Re-writing** is much more than simply preparing a final copy. A good re-writing technique results in a finished piece that says what the writer planned to say. And although this goal sounds obvious, it is not so easy to achieve. These six chapters show you how to make each sentence correct and effective.

Here's an overview of this step-by-step approach to a writing problem — a process for effective writing:

1. Define the writing problem: Think about the **what,** the **who** and the **why** of the writing task.
2. **Brainstorm**: Begin writing sentences, or just parts of sentences, to discover what you think and know.
3. Examine your brainstorming: Build a **working thesis** to direct your material gathering.
4. Gather your **material**: Often your brainstorming will include the necessary details to show your readers what you mean. Just as often, you will need to gather more material by observing, interviewing or using media sources.
5. Control your writing: Write a **statement of purpose** and a **control statement**.
6. Group your ideas: Build a **pattern** which organizes your material.
7. Plan your writing: Use your pattern to construct a **pre-writing plan**.
8. Write your **first draft**.
9. **Review** your first draft: Check for **complete sentences** in **developed paragraphs**.
10. **Re-write** your first draft: Examine each paragraph and, if necessary, re-write sentences for effective **focus, emphasis, subordination** and **parallelism**. Make your **verbs** work and your writing **flow**. Check your **punctuation** and **spelling**. This re-write will result in your **second draft**.
11. Prepare your **final copy**.

Not every writing task requires all these steps. In fact, in Chapter 1 you'll use a shortened process for a writing problem. However, once you've learned to use all these steps, you will be able to overcome any writing challenge you meet. Chapter 15 explains how to use a writing process for some specific writing problems. It takes you through the pre-writing stage for exam questions, how-to and opinion pieces, letters of application and complaint, as well as research papers.

Each chapter offers exercises that encourage you to make the decisions and use the skills of the effective writer. Many of these exercises can be self-marked. (Exercises for which answers are provided at the back of the book are marked with an asterisk(*).) Also, each chapter opens with its purposes clearly stated and closes with a detailed summary of what it has covered. The chapters' final assignments le consecutively through a complete writing process.

Pre-writing

1

Getting Started

Effective Writing

Effective writing is writing that works. It achieves its purpose whether that purpose is describing a new product, explaining how to do something, or convincing someone to grant a job interview. Those whose writing works—effective writers—approach any writing assignment as a problem that is first defined and then solved. Often, the solution requires some effort and good time management. Always, it demands a great deal of thinking within a structured, problem-solving process. This book shows you how to use such a process.

The purposes of this chapter are the following:

1. To summarize a writing process.
2. To introduce the basic elements of every writing problem—the **what**, the **why** and the **who**.
3. To get you thinking about the tools of the craft—words—and how they work.
4. To start you writing using a process.

A Writing Process

In Exercise 1.1 you are going to write a description of an illustration. Let's examine a step-by-step approach for such a problem. Here's the

3

kind of illustration you will be asked to describe:

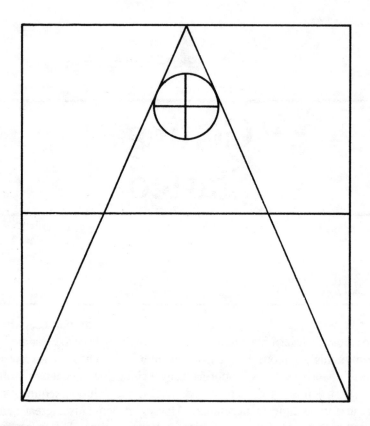

Your first task is to define the writing problem. You know **what** you are writing about, the illustration. But, **why** are you writing about it? What is your purpose? Well, you've been asked to write a description; you want your readers to be able to see the illustration so well that they could draw it after they've read your description. Thus, you need to be very specific about the size of the objects and the relationships between them in the illustration.

And **who** are these readers? In this problem, they are members of your writing class. Once you've established your readership, you can begin to anticipate its needs. What do they, the readers, know about the illustration? What words are they likely to understand? For instance, would everyone know what an isosceles triangle is?

After you've thought carefully about the problem, it's time to start solving it. The first step is to begin using words to express what you mean. This brainstorming can be either a list of words and phrases, or a series of sentences. Don't bother about order. Write what you know. Here's a list for the example:

```
rectangle — acts as a border
          — 9 cm wide by 10 cm high
          — cut in half horizontally with a solid line
 triangle — inside border rectangle
          — base same as bottom of rectangle
          — two sides rise from bottom corners of rectangle,
            meet at center of top line
   circle — inside top of triangle, touches two sides
          — about size of a dime
          — quartered like a pie
```

The next step is to begin ordering and developing your information. In this case, you might use a space order. The information could be presented from the top of the illustration to the bottom, or from the outside of the illustration to the inside. Any space order that makes reading your description easy is the right one. Also, each part of the description needs to be fully developed; add all the information that your readers need. At this stage, you can decide what your paragraph units will be. The result of all this pre-writing is a plan to follow in the writing stage. Often a pre-writing plan looks like this:

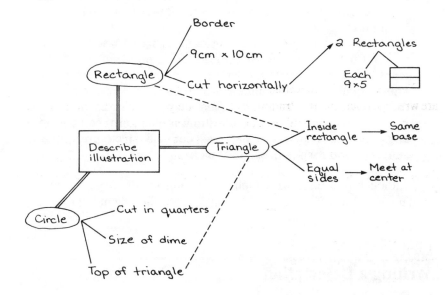

Time now to write your first draft. Write it in the same style that you'd use if you were talking to your readers. Keep them in mind as you follow your plan and write sentences that describe the illustration. Here's an example of a successful first draft:

> A rectangle is the border of the illustration. It's 9 cm wide and 10 cm high. This rectangle is cut in half horizontally by a solid line. The result is two smaller rectangles that measure 9 cm x 5 cm which sit one on top of the other.
>
> Inside the large border rectangle is a triangle. Its base line is the same as the rectangle. The two other sides rise from the bottom left and bottom right corners of the rectangle. These lines are the same length and meet at the center of the top line of the border rectangle.
>
> A circle about the size of a dime is pushed into the top angle of the triangle. This circle is cut in four quarters by two lines forming a cross in the circle.

First drafts are usually quite rough. You need to examine every sentence. Some you'll change so they say what you want correctly and effectively. Also, you'll work to make the piece flow as one smooth composition flows. And of course, you'll check the spelling and punctuation. Finally, you can write your finished piece:

> A 9 cm wide by 10 cm high rectangle acts as the border of the diagram. This rectangle is cut in half horizontally, forming two smaller rectangles. Each one measures 9 cm by 5 cm and they sit one on top of the other.
>
> Inside the large border rectangle is a triangle. Its base line is the same as the rectangle's. Its two other sides rise from the bottom left and right corners of the rectangle. These equal-length lines meet at the center of the top line of the border rectangle and form the triangle's third angle.
>
> A circle about the size of a dime is pushed into the top angle of the triangle. Two lines cut the circle into four quarters and form a cross in the circle.

Although this three-paragraph description seems to work, only the reader can test its effectiveness. Does it describe the original illustration?

Exercise 1.1

Writing a Description

Instructions:

1. Using straight lines and circles, draw an illustration. Keep your illustration simple; use between three and five elements.

2. Write a description of your illustration. Use a writing process to solve the writing problem:

   a) Define the writing problem.
   b) Brainstorm for all the details.
   c) Group the details into paragraph units and then plan how to get from the beginning of your description to the end.
   d) Write a first draft.
   e) Revise and re-write the first draft.
   f) Prepare your final copy.
3. Submit your finished description to a member of your class. Have him or her draw the illustration that you described. See why your writing was effective or almost effective.

Defining the Writing Problem

Every writing problem is defined by its what, why and who:

What are you writing about?
Why are you writing about it?
Who are you writing to?

The what is usually given. Even when your topic is more involved than a concrete, visible illustration, you generally begin a writing assignment knowing something about the topic. Perhaps you don't know as much as you'd like to or as you should, but at least you have an idea. This knowledge, or access to it, is why the assignment is yours. If you are ever assigned a topic you know nothing about, the first step is to go to an encyclopedia and read about that topic.

When you add the why of the assignment, your task becomes clearer. For example, if someone asks you to write about yourself, you might have a difficult time even starting. However, if that someone wants to know about your writing experience, the problem becomes manageable. You don't need to include information about what sports you like, what your favourite snack is, or what television programs you can't stand. Instead, you can begin to list your writing experiences.

When defining the why of the writing problem, think about what your writing is going to accomplish. After they read your piece, will your readers be able to do something, such as bake a cake, or will they understand something, perhaps how the Canadian government works? Do you want them to take some action, for example sending a letter to protest a sexist commercial? Always define your writing problem in terms of a successful solution. Why did you write the description of the illustration? You wanted your readers to see the illustration so well that they could draw it. When you define your writing problem, always express the why as a specific result.

Exercise 1.2

Changing the Why

Instructions:

Write two separate paragraphs about an ordinary lead pencil.

1. Convince people to buy your product.
2. Warn people to keep pencils away from small children.

The third variable of the writing problem is the who. Identifying your readers doesn't mean simply knowing who they are. It means considering what they know about your topic and how you can help them understand your message fully. The following exercise shows that you anticipate your readers' needs all the time.

Exercise 1.3

You and Your Readers

Instructions:

Write about what you did last night.

1. Write first to a close friend.
2. Write to someone who lives in the back country of Australia.

Probably, you'll find that what you wrote to the Australian is more detailed than what you wrote to your friend. Your friend would understand references to events, places and people, but you correctly assumed that the Australian would need more information.

Publishers and editors also attempt to identify and then anticipate their readers' needs and desires. Book publishers spend vast sums trying to determine the market for publishing ventures. Decisions about what to publish and how to edit are based on these surveys. Major magazines are constantly assessing their readership. Most can show a reader profile based on sex, age, occupation, education and income. Both writers and editors use these profiles; what is written and how it is written anticipate the interests of identified readers.

Even though you may not have the same resources as a professional, you can still think about who your readers will be. When you think about your readers' needs and interests and the background knowledge they are likely to have, you form a "reader profile" of your own. Use your "reader profile" to decide how much and what information to include in your writing. Use it also to guide you with word choice.

Brainstorming — Using the Tools of the Craft

Having defined the writing problem, you can now begin to put your ideas down on paper. That means facing the blank page and writing—but not writing for your readers. Instead, you will write for yourself. This next step in the writing process is called brainstorming. When you brainstorm, you write what you know and think and feel about the what of the writing problem. You fill your blank page with words.

And if you are going to use words effectively, you need to consider a fundamental question: what exactly are words? Things you misspell, replies a joker. Perhaps, but here's a more complete explanation. Words are tools that we use to relate our experiences, our thoughts, hopes, fantasies and our opinions. We use words to communicate our world.

Your first responsibility as an effective writer is to communicate to your reader. At a simple theoretical level, the role of words is deceptively straightforward. Any experience can be related using words. The reader reads the words, and if the craft and skill are adequate, the reader understands what has been written.

But, it is rarely that simple. Problems occur when a writer makes incorrect assumptions. Unfortunately, very few words mean the same to everyone. For instance, the word "chair" represents a familiar inanimate object. The exact meaning, however, depends on an individual's experience. For example, in the illustration on the following page the person on the left uses "chair" to communicate an idea. His chair sits in the living room of his house. It is well-padded and is a favourite haunt of the family cat. When the person on the right hears the word, however, the mental image it triggers is quite different. Clearly, the first person has not communicated very well.

This problem of word meaning is even more severe with abstract words that express ideas and opinions. Beauty, freedom and injustice, for example, have different meanings for different people. Yet, effective writers deal with such problems. They build effective sentence structures

Drawing by Kim Page

with specific words. To do this, they must tap their vocabulary reservoir and draw out the words that express exactly what they want to say. Of course, this exactness rarely results from your brainstorming. But, it does start there.

When you brainstorm, you put words down on paper. These words don't have to be in sentences, nor do the ideas expressed have to be in order. But your brainstorming should express your ideas about your writing topic. It should be filled with the words that express those ideas.

Some brainstorming strategies might help. Depending on the writing assignment, consider one or more of these approaches when you brainstorm:

1. Analyze the topic. Take the topic apart and examine each part. Often, this analysis will suggest even more strategies to consider:
   a) How is something made?
   b) How is something used?
   c) Is there an event that centers around the topic? For example, if you were writing about interior decorating, you might use a decorators' convention to direct your brainstorming.
   You might go further and see how the what of your writing assignment fits into a larger picture. For instance, if you are writing about the need for word processing equipment in the office, you might explore how that equipment relates to the entire computer component of the company.
2. Answer questions. Start with the journalistic formula: What? When? Where? Who? Why? Then, explain your answers.
3. Compare your topic to something you know well. Search first for similarities and differences. Then, go further: find the similarities

within the differences and the differences within the similarities. For instance, if I were writing about sailing, which I know little about, I might compare it to golf, which I do know about. If I think about how the two sports are similar, I might write that they can both be enjoyed when you are alone. Then, I can start to list the differences within that similarity — when you sail alone it can be dangerous; when sailing, you are closer to nature; and so on.

4. List the advantages and disadvantages. With some topics, this listing is a good way to begin your brainstorming.

Beginning Your Writing Process

You begin your writing process by first defining the writing problem and then brainstorming for the words and expressions that express your ideas about the topic. This brainstorming can be either a list of words or a collection of sentences. Generally, the latter form is more helpful. The only limits to this brainstorming are those you set when defining the writing problem, the **what**, the **why** and the **who**. Most often, brainstormings tend to ramble and be quite disorganized. However, a good brainstorming will explore your ideas about the topic.

Brainstorming can be the most terrifying step in the writing process. After all, this is when you face the blank page. But remember, brainstorming is for you, not for your readers. The only way to start writing is to put words down on paper.

Final Assignment

Instructions:

Choose one of the following topics. You are writing to members of your class. First, define the writing problem and then brainstorm the topic you've chosen. If necessary, use one of the brainstorming strategies described above. Write for at least a half hour.

1. The most interesting person you've ever met
2. The best job you've ever had
3. The worst job you've ever had
4. Your favourite hobby or sport
5. The best vacation you've ever had

2

Showing What You Mean

Using Your Brainstorming

Effective writing shows your readers what you mean. It doesn't just **tell**:

School's the pits.

It **shows**:

All my marks are Cs or below. I got cut from the basketball team, and my girlfriend's lunch hour is different from mine.

When you brainstormed, you jotted down every thought that came into your head about your topic. Some of these thoughts will give you the details that your piece of writing needs. In fact, your brainstorming creates a set of working papers that you'll use to build an effective piece of writing. When you examine your brainstorming, you'll add to it and you'll get rid of some of it. It serves the same purpose as an artist's rough sketches. Both allow the communicator to explore the problem with the tools of the craft.

This chapter shows you what to look for when you examine your brainstorming. Its purposes are the following:

1. To show how to recognize first-hand experiences and second-hand information—writing that shows.
2. To explain the importance of details to writing that shows.
3. To examine opinions and to explain how to show what you mean by them.

Writing That Shows

When you look over the results of your brainstorming, you will find that your ideas probably come from one of these three sources: your first-hand experiences, second-hand information you remember, or your feelings and opinions. All three categories provide you with some of the material you need for your writing. Let's look at first-hand experiences first.

First-hand Experiences

You experience through your senses with your mind. You see, hear, touch, taste and smell the world. Your mind records these experiences, and when you brainstorm, images, thoughts and sensations return to you. If you communicate these experiences effectively, your readers may be able to imagine what you experienced. So when I write the sentence,

> The chair behind my desk is orange.

I show you the colour of my chair. I can write countless first-hand experiences about my office. They all communicate well because they relate sensory experiences; you can understand all of them. Here's a sampling:

> The telephone in my office is ringing.
> The edge of my desk is ragged and splintered.
> The air conditioning unit emits a burnt rubber smell.
> The coffee tastes like the milk left after the cereal is gone.
> My office is 4.5 m wide and 5.8 m long.
> There are three bookshelves in my office.

First-hand experiences that communicate effectively rely on the fact that we all experience through our senses. Writing that shows tries to make the reader see, hear, touch, taste and smell.

Second-hand Information

You also experience the world through others (even as your readers experience it through you). When you describe what you've read, heard or seen in other media sources, you are using someone else's experiences, second-hand. For many assignments, your brainstorming will be filled with second-hand information. However, to make it communicate effectively, you should give the source of the second-hand information. Cite the print source:

> According to the September 4, 1984 edition of the *Calgary Sun,* Joe Blow paid three million dollars in taxes.

or, the radio source:

On "As It Happens", June 16, 1988, the prime minister talked about her plans for the economy.

or, the television source:

On CTV's current affairs program, which aired on February 28, 1984, a member of an underground terrorist organization talked about training techniques used.

By giving the source along with the information, you are giving your readers the same reading, hearing and seeing experiences.

Adding the Details

To show your readers what you mean, you generally need to provide details. For example, this sentence paints quite a vague picture:

The Great Gatsby, my Old English sheepdog, is lying by my feet.

By adding details to this statement, I can show you the image more clearly:

The Great Gatsby, my Old English sheepdog, is lying by my feet. His back legs are tucked under him and away from me. His front legs are around my left foot and his wet chin is on my right foot. His grey and white hair is hiding his eyes and he is snoring. Gatsby smells like a damp dishcloth.

Details can make your first-hand experiences vivid and show your readers what you experienced. Similarly, details develop your second-hand information. For example, the following sentence leaves many unanswered questions:

Emily Carr was a painter and writer.

Both your purpose and your "reader profile"—the why and the who of the writing problem—would help you choose the details needed to develop this statement.

When you develop a first-hand experience or second-hand information, you add specific details. These details will answer one or more of the following questions:

What?
When?
Where?

How?
To what degree?
Under what conditions?

The more specific you are, the clearer your meaning becomes. Adding the details makes the difference between telling and showing.

Exercise 2.1

Developing Statements

Instructions:

Develop the following simple statements as fully as possible by adding plenty of details. Start answering questions.

1. I am reading a book.
2. A tree stands on a hill.

Explaining Your Opinions

When you brainstorm, you will write down more than first-hand experiences and second-hand information. You will also express opinions. An opinion is neither an experience nor a piece of information, but a judgement. An opinion expresses your individuality. However, an opinion doesn't show; it tells. Here's an example:

> The chair in my office has character.

This statement does not show you my chair. Instead, it tells you what I think of my chair. Only last week, a student looked at my chair and made this comment:

> Rick, that has to be the ugliest chair in the college.

Neither of the above statements shows you what my chair looks like. They tell you that my student and I see the chair differently; each of us expresses an opinion. Here are some more opinions:

> The telephone in my office is a nuisance.
> My desk is dangerous.
> My office stinks.
> The coffee I drink at work is terrible.
> My office is small.
> The bookshelves are too crowded.

Exercise 2.2 *

Recognizing Opinions

Instructions:

Some of the following structures are opinions; others are first-hand experiences or second-hand information. Determine which ones are opinions.

1. College tuition is inexpensive.
2. He was walking along the beach.
3. The cost of living should remain stable.
4. Annual beer consumption in Canada is 45.8 L per individual.
5. The environmentalist said, "Acid rain will be beaten in 10 years."
6. Sara will marry Tom.
7. John is too thin.
8. John weighs 72 kg and is 153 cm tall.
9. Women are terrible drivers.
10. Sheila said she was going to be an actress.
11. My pencil is 14 cm long.
12. The door is locked.
13. He makes me feel inferior.
14. Water boils when heated to 100°C.
15. A four-year-old boy was left alone while his mother visited a neighbour.
16. "Gone with the Wind" should be acclaimed the greatest movie ever made.
17. He has a scar on the left side of his face.
18. According to the *Gazette,* the prime minister said that he thought his marriage was finished.
19. Wayne Gretzky scored last night.
20. The building is going to be finished next week.

There is nothing wrong with expressing opinions. Indeed, they generally abound in a brainstorming, especially when you are struggling to express your ideas. Opinions alone, however, are often vague, confusing or misleading. Therefore, you need to explain your opinions.

Explaining Opinions with First-hand Experiences

One way to explain an opinion is to describe the experience that led you to it. For example, the following sentence is an opinion:

The chair in my office was expensive.

This opinion must be explained or it will mean little to the reader. Therefore, I have to relate the experience that led me to the opinion:

The chair in my office was expensive. It cost $235 plus tax.

Now, you know what I mean when I say that my chair was expensive; I have explained my opinion. Of course, you might not think that $235 plus tax is expensive for a desk chair. But, that's not the point. By adding the experience that led me to the opinion, I communicate what I mean.

Exercise 2.3

Explaining Opinions

Instructions:

For each opinion stated, write a more descriptive statement that explains your meaning—show your readers, rather than tell them, what you mean.

Example:

Opinion: Fred is a big man.
Explanation: At 201 cm and 128 kg, Fred is a big man.

When you've finished, compare what you've written with what others have written. You'll see, by the different explanations, how opinions differ.

1. My car was cheap.
2. There are too many students in the class.
3. She ran a fast race.
4. He can throw a football a long way.
5. He is very short.
6. The building is tall.
7. Our house is very old.
8. The recipe can be prepared quickly.
9. My residence is close to the library.
10. She is a young woman.

Most opinions need more than a single statement to explain them. Instead, they need many details. Here's an example. Suppose I write the following opinion:

He dressed in a strange manner.

Now, I must explain what led me to this opinion; I must show you what I mean. I can't have an opinion of someone without some experience of that person—in this case, what I saw:

> He wore a headpiece that looked like an imitation of the eastern turban, but was really just a dirty white sheet that had been folded and wrapped around his head to cover his forehead. He wore an earring in his left ear, a thin brass loop, and a white turtleneck sweater that was loose at the neck. A leather necklace with a carved tomahawk hung suspended among the folds of a faded pink robe. The robe was knee-length. He wore two different coloured shoes: one was orange and one was pink.

The more details I add, the more meaning I communicate. But remember, I can only show you why I hold the opinion; I can't make you agree with me. You might think this man dresses quite normally.

I could state the following opinion about a house:

> It is an enormous house.

And, I can explain my opinion with the details that show what I mean:

> The house has 43 bedrooms and 47 bathrooms. There are 4 dining rooms and 7 living rooms. The house measures 90 m by 178 m and there are 2000 m² of living space. There is a kitchen in each of the four wings and each kitchen is 10 m by 13 m. The main library is the size of half a football field, and the 3 smaller libraries are as big as the 10 m by 8 m indoor swimming pool in the basement. The ballroom which faces the west gardens can hold 300 guests.

Perhaps I have convinced you, but remember: opinions are not facts. They are an expression of the writer's individuality—a statement of what the writer thinks. As a writer, you have a right to state your opinion, but if you are going to communicate the meaning of the opinion, you have to explain it. Be sure you add the details your reader needs to understand what you are saying. Show your reader what you mean.

Explaining Opinions with Second-hand Information

Often, an opinion will need second-hand information to explain it. Here's an example:

> The cost of a college education is reasonable.

The writer who wrote this opinion probably needs to use more than just first-hand experiences to explain what he means. He might find out facts about the cost of a college education and who pays the entire amount. He might compare his costs to those of students in other provinces. At any rate, he has some work to do before he can communicate what he means.

Predictions and **forecasts** usually require some second-hand information as well. Here's an example from a writer who expresses an opinion of what will be in the future:

> It will rain tomorrow.

Clearly, she can't explain the opinion by relating any first-hand experience of tomorrow, for our experiences are restricted to the present and the past. Opinions about what will happen in the future, called predictions and forecasts, can nevertheless be explained. This particular writer explains her forecast with second-hand information:

> In the past, when weather patterns have moved in the way they are moving now, it has rained within twelve hours. This has happened 75% of the time.

This added information gives her opinion some meaning. Explain your predictions and forecasts in the same manner, with first-hand experiences from the past and second-hand information.

Explaining Opinions by Being More Specific

An opinion of what should be is explained with your reasons for thinking as you do. Consider the following example:

> People who drink should not drive.

To explain this opinion, the writer must first list the reasons why he thinks as he does. He might write down these reasons:

1. Driving while under the influence of alcohol is illegal.
2. The driver's ability to drive is impaired.
3. It is dangerous for others as well as for the driver.

The first reason is factual and may not need further development. The second and third reasons might be considered opinions; the writer should explain these statements with the first-hand experiences or second-hand information that led to the opinions.

Should be opinions express some of our strongest beliefs, but if others are to understand, we must explain them clearly. Thus, to explain your should be opinions, be specific. List why you think as you do. These reasons can then be developed or explained further.

Generalizations make broad, sweeping opinions that are difficult to explain. Here's an example:

> Canadians make the best documentary films in the world.

General statements such as this one sound unreliable. Your readers will ask themselves if you have the knowledge or the authority to make such statements. Since you cannot compare all the documentaries made by Canadians to all other documentaries made in the world—an impossible task—re-write your opinion. Limit it so that it is more specific and you can explain what you mean. For example:

> In the past five years, Canadian documentary films have been well received by critics and audiences around the world.

Such a statement can be explained with second-hand information.

Exercise 2.4

Communicating Opinions

Instructions:

Each of the following statements is an opinion. How would you explain each one?

Remember, explaining an opinion usually means making it more specific and giving your reasons for believing it. When you explain an opinion, you want your readers to understand you, even if they are not convinced by your explanation.

1. College tuition is inexpensive.
2. The cost of living should remain stable.
3. Sara will marry Tom.
4. John is too thin.
5. Women are terrible drivers.
6. Elynor is going to be a great actress.
7. He makes me feel inferior.
8. "Gone with the Wind" should be acclaimed the greatest movie ever made.
9. The building is going to be finished next week.
10. College students never have enough time.

When most writers brainstorm, opinions fill their pages. After a second look, however, the writers discard some of their opinions because they can't explain them adequately or don't want to. Other opinions, on the other hand, are worthy of more consideration, and demand some explanation. Remember to show your readers what you mean. Add details that develop your first-hand experiences and second-hand information. In the same manner, explain your opinions. Write these details on your brainstorming pages as you are reviewing them. This addition of details to your working papers is an important part of your writing process. You are starting to communicate what you mean.

The Process Continues

Examine your brainstorming—you've written some first-hand experiences, some second-hand information and some opinions. All of these ideas need to be developed with more details. Write the necessary details right on your working papers. Remember, you want to **show** your readers, not just **tell** them.

Make sure you examine your opinions closely. If you cannot explain an opinion, or don't want to, get rid of it.

Final Assignment

Instructions:

Examine your brainstorming from Final Assignment, Chapter 1. Identify the first-hand experiences, the second-hand information and the opinions. Get rid of any opinions you can't or don't want to explain.

Suggestion:

Use coloured pens to underline the different structures.

3

Using a
Working Thesis

The Need for Specifics

Effective writing is filled with details—details that develop first-hand experiences and second-hand information, and that explain opinions. Yet, your brainstorming probably didn't contain enough details: that wasn't its purpose. When you were brainstorming, you were just trying to write down everything you know or think or feel about your topic. When you examined your brainstorming, you began to add the details that show your readers what you mean. However, sometimes you will need even more material. How will you get this material?

Deciding what is needed and how to get it are both important steps in the writing process. To make those decisions, you must first use your brainstorming to build a working thesis. This chapter examines this stage of the process. Its purposes are the following:

1. To show why you need a working thesis and how to build one.
2. To explain how to find the material that develops a working thesis.
3. To emphasize that a working thesis may change at this stage of your writing process.

Building a Working Thesis

After you have examined your brainstorming, you should be able to state what you want to say in your piece of writing. That statement is a working thesis. You'll certainly need to keep the why and the who of the writing problem in mind as you work to answer this question:

What do you want to say?

Thus, while your brainstorming lets you explore and discover what you know and think and feel about your topic, the working thesis limits and structures the writing assignment. It structures your writing, for it is a logical, unified statement about your topic. It limits your writing, for it states what ideas you need to develop. Let's examine a couple of working theses and how they are used by writers.

A Professional Example

The people at *Maclean's*, one of Canada's newsmagazines, shared this anecdote in their section called ''Inside Maclean's'':

> One Friday afternoon in early December, a group of Maclean's editors and writers were sitting around arguing the merits of story ideas for near and distant issues... Labour, everyone in the room agreed, was a story. The problem was one of focus... An hour of discussion, some of it heated, ended with a loose working premise—that new elements were at work within the trade union movement making substantial changes in the way workers perceived their jobs and their society. The next step was to see if that premise could be substantiated. A staff writer... was given the assignment and immediately began to wrestle with his interviews, files from staffers and correspondents across the country and the near impossibility of stating all the facts in just 4500 words...
>
> (from *Maclean's*, February 23, 1976)

The working thesis, called in this excerpt a working premise, got the writer going. In this example, it showed the staff writer what he was trying to develop—that there were new elements at work in the trade union movement, and what changes these elements were making in the way workers were perceiving themselves and their jobs. Thus, this working thesis both limited and directed the writer as he wrestled with his information.

A Student Example

Last year I gave a first year business student a writing assignment that was fairly simple. He was to start pre-writing for a paper on a topic relating to the Canadian economy. Discouraged, he shrugged his shoulders and left class. Later that week, he told me he was going to write about the Canadian fishing industry, a topic that he had been studying in another class and had found interesting. The working thesis he developed was the following:

> The Canadian fishing industry is in trouble. Inexpensive imports are reducing the demand for Canadian fish. Fewer fishermen are fishing each year, and the crops are low.

Again, the working thesis limits and directs the writer's process. The student writer now knew what he was doing. He was going to explain his opinion that the industry is in trouble, and develop the ideas expressed by the three statements: imports are reducing demand, fewer fishermen are fishing, and the crops are low.

Exercise 3.1

Building Your Working Thesis

Instructions:

Build a working thesis for each of the topics listed below. Don't forget to define the writing problem first: the what, the why and the who. You may need to brainstorm as well.

1. Consumers' rights
2. Sexual equality
3. Protecting the environment
4. Computer technology
5. Fashion
6. Censorship
7. Television

Getting the "Stuff"

Gathering the material that develops your working thesis is the legwork part of the process. The beginning professional writers I work with just can't believe the amount of plain time-consuming slogging that's required to put together a well-developed piece of writing. But, the thinking and reading and talking and listening and thinking again are just exactly what combine to make an effective piece.

As you saw in Chapter 2, you have plenty of ideas and details about a topic in your head. Sometimes this material is enough for your piece of writing. Other times, you will need to research. This research can take several forms—observing, interviewing or using media sources.

Observing

When your working thesis calls for material that you don't have, seek the information directly, if possible. Observe the person, place or thing you are writing about.

Both novelists and historical writers require background information for scenes and situations. Arthur Hailey spends years pre-writing his books. He reportedly spent thousands of hours in the lobby of Toronto's Royal York Hotel while preparing his novel *Hotel*. Pierre Berton travels to the scenes of his popular histories and observes the wildlife, vegetation and terrain.

Business and technical writers are forever observing. They create experiments and surveys to generate information directly, or observe the subject matter at firsthand, often over a period of time.

Exercise 3.2

Observing

Instructions:

1. Find an interesting-looking person, someone you don't know.
2. Observe this person for a period of time.
3. Write a description of the person and try to show your readers the impression you had of that person.

Interviewing

Sometimes, you'll be able to talk to someone who has had experiences that offer the material you need. An interview can be short and informal, or longer and much more structured. You might talk to someone on the telephone or mail the interviewee a questionnaire. However, when you interview someone, always prepare. Know what you are after and don't waste the interviewee's time. When you are preparing to interview, keep these guidelines in mind:

1. Define the purpose of the interview. Make sure you can state specifically what information you want to gain.
2. Do some background reading to find out about the subject. An encyclopedia is a good place to get general background information.
3. Write out some questions that you'll ask the person you are interviewing.

When you actually interview the person, listen actively. Ask questions that come from the material you've heard. Try to make the situation as comfortable and natural as you can.

Exercise 3.3

Interviewing

Instructions:

1. Find someone in your class who has an unusual hobby or interest that you know nothing or little about.
2. Prepare yourself and then interview the person.
3. Write a three-paragraph piece about the hobby or interest.

Using Media Sources

Books, magazines, film strips, computer information banks as well as television, film and radio are all sources of information. However, finding the best material to support your working thesis can be difficult. Using media sources is almost a separate discipline within the craft of writing. Here are some tips that will help you look for the material you need.

1. **Try to find as many sources as you can.** Search for a variety of sources, especially if you cannot get the information by observing or interviewing. Remember, if you rely on only one source, you may be summarizing only one other writer or speaker.
2. **Look for the most recent information.** This is especially important if your topic is current. For example, if you were using this working thesis,

   There have been many developments in computer technology in the last two years.

   and then used sources published in the 1970s, your information would be hopelessly out-of-date. The most up-to-date information would likely be in magazines and computer banks.
3. **Use your own words.** Don't be a copying machine. Express the ideas in your own language. Only when you are recording another's opinion or stating statistics and other numerical facts should you quote information word for word. If you cite a source in this manner, indicate that you are using a quotation.
4. **State what sources you've used.** The reader can check your information only by going to your sources. Keep track of what book,

magazine or media production is the source of your material. Indicate when it was published or produced, who the writers or editors are, where it was published and on what pages you found the information. This data will be used in footnotes, in a bibliography, which is a list of sources, or in both. Any style guide will show you the correct way to handle footnotes and to build a bibliography.

5. **Think when you research.** Keep thinking about how the material you find will affect your working thesis.

Exercise 3.4

Using Media Sources

Instructions:

State what media sources you would use to research the following working theses.

1. The two-handed backhand has changed the game of tennis.
2. The living room of the celebrity's mansion in Los Angeles is spectacular.
3. The number of people killed on the nation's highways has decreased since the speed limit was lowered.
4. The XYZ Company's new product is poorly designed.
5. The early settlers in New Brunswick had a hard time.

Changing Your Working Thesis

Getting the "stuff" to develop a working thesis may force you to change that statement. Often, you will discover new information; perhaps while researching you will find a new angle, something more effective. Or perhaps you will redefine the who, why or what of the writing problem. Changing a working thesis happens often. The people at *Maclean's* discuss this situation in another "Inside Maclean's" column:

> Investigative journalists . . . usually go into stories with a working thesis, but almost inevitably the thesis is amended (or destroyed) by the time they are ready to write.
>
> (from *Maclean's*, April 5, 1976)

Here are two examples that show why a working thesis can change. In the first, a writer discovers some facts that alter the way she interprets a situation. She begins with this piece of information, and uses it as her working thesis:

> The mayor has received money from a local contractor.

When searching for more information, however, she discovers the following:

> On June 7, 1984, Bill Lowly, President of GHY Construction, gave Miss March, the mayor's secretary, $300 in cash.
>
> Miss March is the secretary-treasurer of the Young People's Charity Foundation.
>
> The money was donated to the Foundation by the employees of GHY Construction to help defray the costs of a picnic that the young people are planning for the residents of the Senior Citizen's home.

The situation that the writer first suspected didn't exist. Instead, she finds a human interest story about a group of construction workers and young people. Clearly, she has to change her working thesis to include this new information.

This kind of rethinking is even more common when a writer sets out to explain an opinion. (This is especially true when we adopt opinions from others without any real investigation on our part.) In the second example, a college student discovers that his opinion is unfounded. He wants to prove the following working thesis:

> The people who graduated from XY College last year have jobs that pay poorly and that they dislike.

He tries to explain this opinion, but learns the following statistics when researching:

> 332 students graduated last year.
>
> 307 have jobs in the same field as the one they studied in college.
>
> The lowest salary reported by the 289 graduates who responded to the questionnaire was $7 800.
>
> The highest salary reported was $20 200.
>
> The average salary was $14 830.
>
> 247 of the respondents said that they had supervisory responsibilities.
>
> 95% said they thought their futures looked promising.
>
> 57 said that they were unhappy with their jobs.

The writer's original opinion no longer expresses what the statistics reveal. Clearly, he needs to rethink his writing assignment and what he wants to say. (This example also shows what happens when you don't do some preliminary research before writing about something you know nothing about.)

Your working thesis is a starting point; it can change as you gather the material necessary to express its ideas. Of course, your material gathering must end, eventually. At some point, based on the variables of the writing problem (the who, the why and the what), you will have enough of the ''stuff.'' Think of your readers and how much they need to know. Think about your reasons for writing. With the who and the why in mind, work to get the material necessary to communicate what you want to say.

The Process Continues

1. Use your brainstorming to build a working thesis. This working thesis states what you want to say to your readers for your purposes. It is a unified, logical statement that limits your material gathering, for it states what ideas you are going to develop.
2. Write details that develop the working thesis. Some of these details will be in your brainstorming. Gather additional material by observing, interviewing, or using media sources.
3. Keep examining your working thesis. There are three reasons why you should change it:
   a) You find new information that changes your opinions.
   b) You discover a different approach to the topic.
   c) You need to redefine the what, the why or the who of the writing problem.

Final Assignment

Instructions:

Use one of the working theses you wrote for Exercise 3.1. Gather material to develop that working thesis. Your writing assignment should be about 1000 words, so try to collect more than 1000 words' worth of information. Remember, you are only pre-writing. Do not write the assignment; just gather the ''stuff.''

4

Controlling
Your Writing

Using Your Material

Effective writing is controlled. Every paragraph and every sentence advances the writer's purpose. Writing that isn't controlled, on the other hand, has no real direction. It rambles and drifts from one paragraph to the next.

How do effective writers pull their material into a controlled piece of writing? First, they return to the three variables of the writing problem, the who, the why and the what, and express the why and the what in very precise terms. This chapter will show how to express these variables. Its purposes are the following:

1. To emphasize the importance of a statement of purpose and to explain how to write one.
2. To show how writing is controlled by the statement of purpose and by a control statement.
3. To give guidelines for writing a control statement.

A Statement of Purpose

When you first define the writing problem, you express the why as a specific result. Thus, if you are preparing an application letter, you are writing to get a job interview. If you are writing an essay for a class, you want to receive an acceptable grade. The why of every writing problem can be expressed as a successful result.

You have now started following a writing process. You have gathered the material that will make your writing effective. Your task now is to combine what you've learned by gathering material and your thoughts about your readers into a statement that expresses exactly why you are writing the piece — a statement of purpose. A statement of purpose answers this question:

Why are you writing the piece?

The question is answered very specifically.

Begin the statement with one of three primary purposes: to describe, to inform, or to persuade. Second, identify your readers. Finally, state what you are describing, informing about, or arguing. Here are three examples:

To describe to my friend the hotel where I'm spending my holidays.

To inform my teacher about why I didn't get my assignment completed on time.

To persuade readers of the local newspaper that smoking should be banned in public places.

Often, a successful statement of purpose combines more than one purpose. For example, a student writer is pre-writing an article for the school newspaper about facilities in the women's residence. She has followed her own writing process and gathered material. In her opinion, the facilities are inadequate. She has also interviewed school officials who told her that there are no plans for improving the residence. The writer puts together her information and her decisions in this statement of purpose; this is why she is writing:

To describe to readers of the school newspaper the inadequate facilities available in the women's residence and to inform that school officials are not planning to improve the facilities.

Exercise 4.1

Writing Statements of Purpose

Instructions:

Find three magazine articles about any topics you choose. Read each article and then write the statement of purpose that controlled the article.

Bring your articles and your statements of purpose to class. Have others in the class read the articles and evaluate your statements of purpose.

A Control Statement

While a statement of purpose states why you are writing, a control statement states what you are going to say to achieve your purpose. A control statement can be the same as a working thesis; the difference is that a control statement is written after the material gathering step of your process. A control statement is a logical, unified statement that summarizes your material. Writing a control statement is a crucial step in your writing process, for the statement achieves two purposes:

1. It states what you are going to say in your piece.
2. It controls the piece of writing.

Here's an example of how the statement of purpose and the control statement are linked, and how they control a piece of writing. My car, which my wife has named Florabelle, is a fine car. It's gone over 95,000 miles and has been relatively trouble-free. It's fun to drive; it has bucket seats, a racing-type steering wheel, full instrumentation and a five-gear stick shift. Unfortunately, it is starting to fall apart, rusty piece by rusty piece.

When I bought Florabelle, it was royal blue, but today the blue has faded and is pocked with dirty orange. These large and small rust spots cover the doors and fenders, but no part of Florabelle is rust-free. In too many places, the rust has eaten the body, leaving growing holes, and when I close the hatch-back, more of the car falls to the road. Just the impact of closing the doors is enough to dislodge more of the car's body.

It doesn't really bother me to drive such a car, but lately people have been giggling at me and at the state of my Florabelle. You can understand then why I've decided to have a body job and a new paint job. I've shopped around and the best price I can find is about $700.

I've also decided to ask both the car dealer and the manager of the rust protection company that rust-proofed the car when I bought it to contribute to Florabelle's restoration. I anticipate that both these local business people will at least read my argument. They are aware of the problem and are also very concerned with their customer relations. Hence, with these decisions about purpose and readers made, I can write my statement of purpose:

> To persuade both the car dealer and the manager of the rust protection company to each pay one quarter of the cost of a body job and paint job for my car

My next step is to write my control statement. I must state precisely what

I am going to say to my readers. After all, I want them to spend $175; I'd better have a good argument. I write the following:

My car has had all scheduled maintenance and rust inspections and has been driven and used in a normal fashion, yet it is rusting away. Contributing to the body and paint job is a good advertisement for both the dealer and the rust protection company.

These four ideas have to be developed, of course. And thus, they control my writing. I will use only material that expands on these four statements:

My car has had all scheduled maintenance and rust inspections.
My car has been driven and used in a normal fashion.
My car is rusting away.
Contributing to the body and paint job is a good advertisement for both the dealer and the rust protection company.

Without my control statement, I wouldn't know what I was going to say in my letters. I would run the risk of rambling and of writing material which wouldn't help me achieve my purpose.

Writing Your Control Statement

Writing a control statement causes many problems for many writers. You are actually forced to state what you are going to say. When you write a control statement, consider these six guidelines:

1. **Make the subject the first word or words of your statement.** For example, a writer's statement of purpose might be the following:

   To describe to readers of the fan magazine the living room of the celebrity's house.

   The living room is the subject of the piece of writing. Thus, when the writer writes the control statement, she presents these words first:

   The living room of the celebrity's house...

2. **Your control statement must be a statement; it cannot be a question.** The writer mentioned above might state what she saw:

   The living room of the celebrity's house is filled with pine furniture.

   Or, she might give her opinion of what she saw:

   The living room of the celebrity's house is very impressive.

   Both these control statements say something about the living room.

However, the following question could not control her piece of writing:

Have you ever seen a room where you would like to stay forever?

Although this question might serve as a successful introduction, it is not a control statement because it does not make a statement.

3. **A control statement tightly summarizes the material you are using.** It must be a statement that your material can develop directly. Therefore, the following examples could not be used as control statements, for they are too general:

The living room of the celebrity's house should be a room in a museum.

The living room of the celebrity's house is more impressive than the rooms in museums.

*Exercise 4.2 ***

Recognizing Impossible Control Statements

Instructions:

Determine which of the following could not act as control statements. Re-write them so that they could control a piece of writing.

1. I think that smoking is harmful to your health.
2. Flying hang-gliders.
3. School cafeterias set their prices too high for students on a budget.
4. Hagood Hardy's "The Homecoming" is the best piece of music ever composed.
5. Will Russia and the United States ever achieve détente?
6. Ratepayers groups are changing municipal politics in Canadian towns and cities.
7. The minister of finance should introduce a new budget.
8. Evidence suggests that heart attacks are caused by stress.
9. Marijuana will be legal someday.
10. If you want a really good time, come out and cheer the school football team this Saturday.

The guidelines continue:

4. **A control statement can have more than one subject.** It can state more than one idea that you are going to develop.

How large a control statement is depends on the statement of purpose. Here's an example of this link between a statement of purpose and a control statement. A writer might write this statement of purpose:

To describe to readers of the school newspaper the inadequate facilities available in the women's residence, and to inform that school officials are not planning to improve the facilities.

Her control statement states what she is going to say to achieve these purposes:

The living quarters, the recreational areas, and the telephone service in the women's residence are unsatisfactory, and school officials have stated that they are not planning to improve the situation.

Her control statement has four subjects:

the living quarters in the women's residence
the recreational areas
the telephone service
school officials

The first three subjects are the facilities she will describe to her readers. The fourth subject comes from her second purpose, to inform about the school officials.

The control statement states **what** the writer is going to say about her subjects. Her piece of writing will develop these statements:

The living quarters in the women's residence are unsatisfactory.
The recreational areas in the women's residence are unsatisfactory.
The telephone service in the women's residence is unsatisfactory.
School officials have stated that they are not planning to improve the situation.

5. **A statement of purpose may require that you answer the question *how* or *why* in the control statement.** For example, a writer might make this statement of purpose:

To inform the manager of the school cafeteria about the lineups and why they exist.

The control statement must state what the writer will say to achieve this purpose:

Lineups are long and common in peak periods. Not enough food is prepared beforehand and the checkout system can't handle the volume.

However, this control statement does not explain explicitly why there are long lineups. If the word *why* occurs in the statement of purpose, the control statement must answer the question. Use *because* to link the reasons to the effect more clearly:

Lineups are long and common in peak periods *because* not enough food is prepared beforehand and *because* the check-out system can't handle the volume.

Similarly, if the word *how* occurs in the statement of purpose, the control statement must answer this question also. For example, a writer might make this statement of purpose:

To inform the class about how Carol Tremblay became an effective writer.

The writer has decided to write about Ms. Tremblay's being an effective writer and how she became one. The control statement will present the following information:

Carol Tremblay has become an effective writer.
She studied other writers.
She worked at the craft of writing.

However, these statements don't explain how Carol Tremblay became an effective writer. Use *by* to link the ways and means more clearly:

Carol Tremblay has become an effective writer *by* studying other writers and *by* working at the craft of writing.

6. **A control statement can be more than one sentence.** Your most important task is to state what your piece of writing is going to say. The control statement must be precise, logical and simple, so don't force your ideas in to one muddled and awkward statement.

The Process Continues

1. When you have all the material that you need, review your decisions about the what, the who, and the why of the writing problem.

2. Write a statement of purpose.

   It states specifically **why** you are writing to your readers.
   It begins with a primary purpose:
      to describe
      to inform
      to argue (or persuade).
   It identifies your readers.
   It states what you are describing, or informing about, or arguing.

3. Write your control statement.

It is a pre-writing tool.

It states **what** you are going to write to achieve your purpose.

Your control statement summarizes the material you have gathered. It is a logical, unified statement that expresses the ideas your writing will develop.

Final Assignment

Instructions:

Using the information you gathered for Final Assignment, Chapter 3, review your writing problem and then submit your statement of purpose, control statement and information.

5

Building a Pattern

Planning Your Writing

Effective writing is planned. Paragraphs and sentences are ordered to lead the reader from beginning to end. To help order their information, most effective writers build pre-writing plans. Such plans are similar to architects' blueprints: both plans specify where all the details belong.

Before an architect creates a blueprint, he or she makes preliminary drawings. The architect uses these drawings to work out how specific parts of the building relate to each other. Writers follow a similar process. Your next task is to build a working structure—a pattern of the information you've collected. This chapter examines this important skill of patterning. Its purposes are the following:

1. To show how to build a pattern of your information.
2. To explain how a pattern can be used to check your previous decisions.

What's a Pattern?

A pattern arranges your information logically. Here's an example. A writer writes the following statement of purpose and control statement:

> To describe to readers of the fan magazine the living room of the celebrity's house.
>
> The living room of the celebrity's house is very impressive.

38

Her information is patterned in this way:

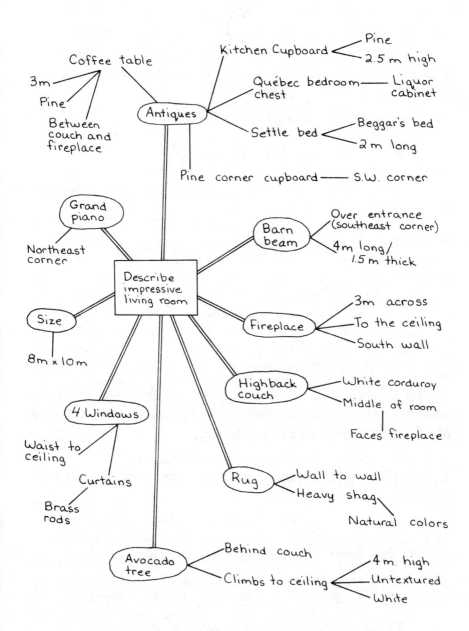

The information that is circled notes what the writer saw. These observations support the opinion expressed in the control statement. Explaining why the living room is impressive is the central purpose that controls the entire pattern. Further details are added to develop the first-hand experiences. Each detail attaches to a specific observation.

This pattern illustrates the basic rules of patterning:

1. The statement of purpose and control statement control the pattern.
2. Every entry develops or supports a broader entry.

Here's a section of the pattern showing this principle:

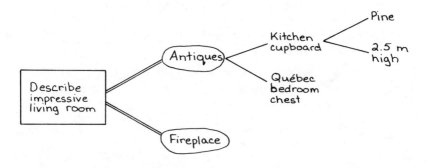

The pattern develops like the limbs of a tree. Everything grows into more and more details. Yet the purpose anchors all the points and holds the information together.

How to Build a Pattern

When your control statement is longer than a single statement, break it apart. Each part will become a main branch of the pattern. For example, consider the following statement of purpose and control statement:

> To describe the inadequate facilities in the women's residence and to tell students that school officials are not planning to improve the facilities.

> The living quarters, the recreational areas and the telephone service in the women's residence are unsatisfactory, and school officials have stated that they are not planning to improve the situation.

These statements are used to build the skeleton of the writer's pattern:

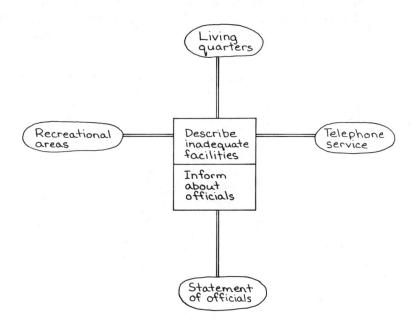

The writer can now build her pattern, adding information as it develops her four statements.

After breaking your control statement apart, your next task is to build your information into a pattern. Let's examine part of one writer's process and follow this patterning stage all the way through.

The writer is the assistant to the public relations director of an alternate energy company. Recently, the company has been receiving a number of complaints about the specialized and technical nature of their information on solar energy. The writer's supervisor and she decide that a simple information report might solve the problem. This report will be handed out at the company's information booth at an upcoming trade show.

The writer defines the writing problem. She writes a working thesis and then gathers information. Finally she writes the following statement of purpose:

> To inform visitors to the information booth about solar energy—how it works, its advantages, uses and costs.

Her control statement then specifies what she is going to write in the report:

Solar energy systems use the sun's energy. Solar energy has various advantages and uses, and its costs are reasonable.

This control statement breaks apart to form the skeleton of her pattern:

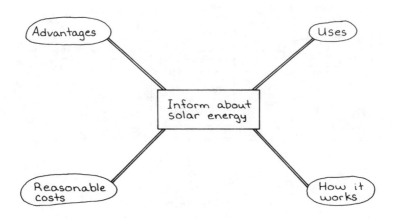

Our writer's next task is to build her information into a pattern. Here are the results of her research (she has noted what source she used to find each piece of information).

Source 1
—Swimming pool and water heating system kits cost between $1000 and $1500. Installation costs range from $500 to $1000.

—Active solar energy systems have four common elements. Each system has components which
  1. collect the heat
  2. store the heat
  3. distribute the heat
  4. control the system.

—There are two kinds of active space systems. One uses anti-freeze and is called a hot liquid system. The second stores heat in rocks which are generally kept in a below ground pit. This system is called a hot air system.

—A house designed with passive solar heating in mind has
1. large recessed windows facing south.
2. an overhang that allows the solar radiation to penetrate during the winter but shades the house during summer mid-day hours.
3. evergreens planted on the north side to minimize wind exposure.
4. trees that lose their leaves planted on the south side to provide shade in summer and allow the sun's rays to penetrate during the winter.

—Solar energy can be used to supply a home's water heating energy requirements. Solar water heating systems come in complete packages which can be purchased and added to your house. All that is needed is 6 m^2 of south-facing roof.

Source 2

—Solar energy offers environmental advantages. Solar energy, unlike fossil fuels, poses no threat to the environment.

—In active systems, heat from the sun is collected in a collector. These collectors are generally mounted on a southern roof; they function like a furnace in a basement.

—Solar energy can be used to heat homes and buildings.

—Most homes can make use of passive solar heating by having drapes and blinds on south-facing windows open during the day and closed at night.

—Even though solar energy is more expensive than other forms right now, two trends are evident:
1. Fossil fuels will become more expensive.
2. Solar energy systems will become less expensive.

Source 3

—The supply is limitless; no foreign government can cut off the supply of sunlight.

—Experts predict that solar energy can provide between 25% and 70% of Canada's energy requirements. This range reflects demand in certain parts of the country.

—Millions of dollars are being spent by governments and companies to develop solar energy.

—Solar energy can heat swimming pools. This is an ideal use of solar power because such heating is required during the summer months when the sun is the strongest. Also, the system is required to raise the water's temperature only 5-10° C.

—A passive solar system puts solar radiation to use without the mechanical equipment contained in an active system. There are no tanks and no bins to store the heat and no fans or pumps to insure the movement.

—A commercial active system can run from $5000 to $9000 for a house of 140 to 170 m^2.

Exercise 5.1*

Building a Pattern

Instructions:

Use the solar energy information to build a pattern.

1. Reduce each entry to key words.
2. If you think information fits in more than one place, make a decision about the best use of that material.
3. If material doesn't fit into your pattern, it doesn't belong in the piece of writing. In this exercise, one piece of information does not fit.

Using Your Pattern

Patterns are built to be used. There is no better time to think about your readers and to decide whether you have enough information and whether the piece of writing will achieve its purpose. When you examine your pattern, keep anticipating how your readers will react. Make sure that you have developed your material adequately. Try to anticipate any unanswered questions that your readers might have. Then answer them, again right on your pattern. In fact, use your pattern as working papers. Give yourself lots of room. A pattern that is cramped and crowded and that cannot be examined is not a satisfactory working structure.

These are only suggestions, not rules, but they can better prepare you to use your pattern to order your writing.

The Process Continues

On the following page, you will find the pattern that I used in writing this chapter.

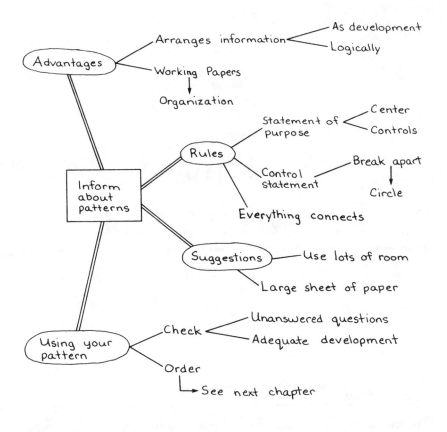

Final Assignment

Instructions:

Build a pattern using the statement of purpose, control statement and information that you submitted in Final Assignment, Chapter 4.

6

Building a
Pre-writing Plan

Organizing Your Writing

Effective writing is organized. It flows logically from its beginning, through the middle, to the end. It must because a written piece is not like a photograph, a painting, or a piece of ceramics; the reader can't see the whole thing in an instant. Thus, effective writing must hold its readers from the beginning to the end. To do so, each part of the composition must flow purposefully to the next part.

Effective writers plan this flow. Using a complete pattern of their material, they build a pre-writing plan. This completed plan is like an architect's blueprint; it shows what their paragraphs will be, how best to order the information in each paragraph and how best to order the paragraphs. This chapter looks at these final pre-writing decisions. Its purposes are the following:

1. To introduce the idea and properties of a paragraph.
2. To explain how to use a pattern to order the meaning within your paragraphs.
3. To introduce the standard orders of development for entire pieces of writing.

Your Pattern and Paragraphs

A paragraph is a unit of meaning that is controlled by a **topic sentence**. Generally, the topic sentence is presented first. The remaining sentences develop the topic sentence. Here's an example:

> The tariff on books coming into Canada was never especially onerous: just ten per cent, added to the wholesale cost of books at the border. Since the wholesale cost is about half of retail, this meant that the tariff—as it worked its way up the chain of book distribution—cost us somewhere between five and ten cents on every dollar we paid. In all it came to something more than $10 million a year.
>
> (from "A Question of Duty" by Robert Fulford, published in *Saturday Night*, July, 1982)

Sometimes, especially when the paragraph explains an opinion, the topic sentence is stated last:

> I sit and cry when I read such stories. "I picked the little guy up and begged him to stop crying," a 23-year-old Toronto man recently admitted with regard to the death of his six-month-old son. "But he just cried louder and I hit him on the head with my fist. Then he stopped crying. He passed out and started to vomit." A little girl dies of massive blows to the stomach; an autopsy on a 14-month-old boy reveals two arm fractures, four broken ribs, a fractured wrist and several skull fractures. The list is seemingly endless—indeed, at least *one million* children in North America are abused or maltreated each year, an estimated 2,000 of whom die as a direct result! In an April, 1981, report on child abuse authorized by the Canadian government, homicide was found to be the fourth major cause of death among Canadian children aged 1 to 5. And according to all reports, these horrifying statistics are on the rise. Canada, it seems, is losing its fight against child abuse. More to the point, innocent children are losing their lives.
>
> (from "Suffer the innocent children" by Joy Fielding, *Maclean's*, October 26, 1981)

The paragraph is the structural link between the pre-writing stage and the writing stage of the process. For, although the paragraph is clearly a prose structure, you can determine what it will be from your pattern. Look at this example. Here's the statement of purpose:

> To inform my friend about the great holiday I'm having in Freeport.

The writer's draft has three paragraphs. Each circled entry becomes the subject of a topic sentence. The details that develop each topic sentence are ordered in separate paragraphs:

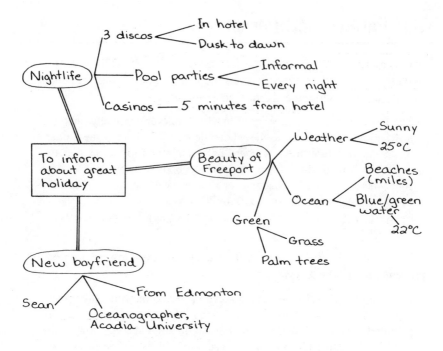

Freeport is a beautiful place. Every day has been sunny
and the temperature has been at least 25 degrees. Also,
everything is so green. The grass and the palm trees hurt my
snow-blinded eyes. Of course, the sandy beaches aren't green,
but they do stretch for miles beside the blue-green ocean. By
the way, the water temperature is above 22 degrees.

When it's too dark to see the beauty, you have lots of excitement. The hotel has three discos that open after supper and
don't close until dawn. There's always a pool party beside the
outside bar, and if you want to leave the hotel, there's a casino
with one-armed bandits, roulette and blackjack tables just a
five-minute walk away.

And by the way, I have a new friend to walk with. His name
is Sean and he's originally from Edmonton. Sean is an
oceanographer who works for Acadia University. Of course,
because of his job, we often walk and look at the ocean—every
night. Can't wait to see you and tell you all.

When a section of your pattern is too large to become a single
paragraph, split it. Determine topic sentences as well as the details that
develop each topic sentence. Here's another example. One section of the
solar energy pattern becomes three paragraphs:

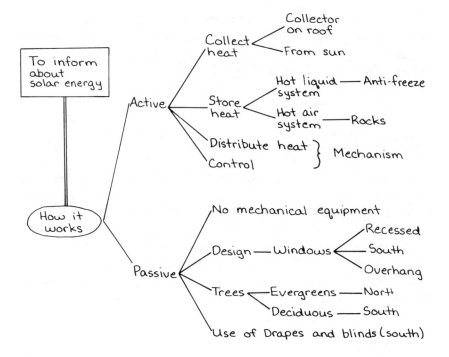

Both active and passive solar systems use the sun's energy. In an active system, there are four components. Heat from the sun is collected in a collector which is usually mounted on a southern roof. This heat is then stored in either anti-freeze or rocks. The first system is called a hot liquid system; the second is a hot air system. Both systems have mechanisms which distribute the heat and control the system.

A passive system, on the other hand, uses solar radiation without this mechanical equipment. There are no tanks or bins, no fans or pumps. Instead, the house is designed in a special way. You'll find large recessed windows facing south. These will have an overhang that allows the sun to penetrate in the winter, but shades the house in the summer.

Most homes can use passive solar heating. During the winter, make sure you open your drapes and blinds on the south during the day and close them at night. Also, you can plant deciduous trees along the southern side. These will provide shade in the summer, but will allow heat to penetrate in the winter. You can also plant evergreens on the north side of the house to minimize wind exposure.

In the above example, each paragraph presents a developed idea. The writer knows to separate the material on passive solar energy into two paragraphs because there are two ideas. The first compares passive solar energy to active solar energy. The second explains how all of us can use passive solar energy.

Ordering Meaning Within Your Paragraphs

Once you've established the paragraph units, your task is to order the paragraph's information. You've already seen that a topic sentence can be presented effectively either first or last. Similarly, all the details in the paragraph can be ordered to make the paragraph effective.

Generally, paragraphs follow a standard paragraph order. The material you've gathered to develop the topic sentence usually lends itself to one of these orders. Examine your pattern to decide the best order for the information in each paragraph.

Time Order

A time order presents meaning through time—either going forward or going backward. Details are ordered as they happened, or as they should happen, for instance when you are giving instructions. In the following example, the writer presents events from the life of C. D. Howe, in chronological order:

His New England heritage as a doer with a hard-rock belief in himself and his capacities remained the dominant strain in Howe's character. Born at Waltham, Mass., in 1886, Howe graduated from MIT in 1907 and stayed on as an engineering instructor for a few months until his professor recommended both him and a fellow graduate for a full-fledged lectureship at Dalhousie University. They tossed a coin to see who would apply, and Howe won. After five years in Halifax, he moved to the Lakehead as chief engineer with the Board of Grain Commissioners and three years later established his own engineering firm. During the next decade and a half, Howe built grain storage facilities worth $125 million at harbours from Canada to Argentina, including the Port Arthur Saskatchewan Pool Seven, the largest grain elevator in the world.

(from *The Canadian Establishment*, Vol. I by Peter C. Newman, used by permission of The Canadian Publishers, McClelland and Stewart Limited, Toronto)

Space Order

Space order is used to show the physical relationship of things to one another. When you organize your material according to space, establish a specific order. Move from left to right, or from right to left; from near to far, or from far to near; from top to bottom, or from bottom to top. Many other specific space orders are possible; no single one is correct. But, you must establish a consistent space order so that your readers can follow your description. Notice how each of the following three paragraphs uses space order:

> At Adams River last October, the group I was with had followed the sockeye all the way from the mouth of the Fraser. About 150 kilometres to the east, the peaceful Fraser Valley closes into the mountains at Hope, and the river turns north into the awesome Fraser Canyon. Halfway up, at Hell's Gate, an airtram ride across the narrow canyon gives a good view of the world's largest manmade "fishways," which help the fish pass safely upstream.
>
> Dramatic changes of scenery continue upriver. At Lytton, where we turn from the brown-watered Fraser to the surprising blue of the Thompson, there's a sudden shift from forested canyons to a stark arid landscape of scrub pine and sagebrush. Thompson country is the land of saddle soap and gunsmoke, of long-ago gold rushes and modern ranches.
>
> Further east past Kamloops, we're back again to the full and glorious colours of autumn. The long arms of Shuswap Lake push their shores into layers of hills rising blue and purple from the deep water. On its north arm, Shuswap meets Adams Lake, and here our struggling sockeye find the clear shallow streams of their birth.
>
> (from "Follow That Salmon" by Carol Ferguson, published in *Canadian Living*, September, 1983)

Order of Importance

Often, you will order a paragraph by starting with the most important point. If you follow with the next most important and so on, you are using a **decreasing** order of importance. Starting with the least important point creates an **increasing** order of importance.

> The government sponsored plan if altered and expanded could be an ideal retirement scheme for women. It's portable and able to accommodate that large number of women who work for many different employers as they weave in and out of the work force. It would include

part-time workers, of whom seventy-two per cent are women. And it could include homemakers.

(from "Affirmative Actions" by Maggie Siggins, published in *Toronto Life*, June, 1982)

General to Particular Order

First, the most general information is presented. (This is usually the topic sentence.) Subsequent details become increasingly specific. This order is often used to present ideas that are at first simple and then become more complex. Sometimes this order is used when the information moves from the familiar to the unfamiliar.

Skin is a complex structure that experts now view as a system with a number of functions under different controls, each working together. Approximately two millimeters thick and weighing roughly six pounds, it consists of three layers: the epidermis (which you can see), the dermis (which lies underneath) and the hypodermis or subcutaneous tissue.

(from "Summerizing Skin Care: Hot Weather How-Tos" by Charlotte Empey, first published in *Flare*, July 1982)

Cause and Effect Order

The topic sentence states the effect—what happened. The body of the paragraph gives the causes or the reasons why it happened.

The use of paper currency (dollar bills, fives, tens, ...) has become widespread because it has many conveniences as a medium of exchange. Currency is easily carried and stored away. By the printing of more or fewer zeros on the face value of the bill, a great or small amount of value can be embodied in a light transportable medium of little bulk. By the use of decimal points it can be made as divisible as we wish. By careful engraving, the value of the money can be made easily recognizable and can be protected from counterfeiting and adulteration. The fact that private individuals cannot create it at will in unlimited amounts keeps it scarce, i.e., an economic rather than a free good.

(from *Economics*, Canadian Edition, by Paul Samuelson and Anthony Scott, published by McGraw-Hill Ryerson Limited, 1966)

Comparison and Contrast Order

Often when you are explaining a topic that is unfamiliar to your readers, you will contrast or compare that topic with another topic that your readers are familiar with. When you are showing how two things are similar, you are comparing. When you are showing how two things differ, you are contrasting. Very effective paragraphs can be ordered around a comparison and contrast technique when the reader knows little about the topic:

> Can this be the same Salvation Army that this month (June 24 to 28) celebrates its Canadian centenary at a giant congress in Winnipeg? Well, not quite. Yesterday's Army was small, struggling, evangelical. Most of its congregation were former outcasts of society who had been converted. Today, many of the Salvation Army's 130,000 Canadian members are third, fourth, even fifth-generation Salvationists, middle-class, born into the movement. Many are "adherents" who don't wear uniforms but attend corps meetings on Sundays and may or may not leave it at that. In the 1880s, Salvationists who beat their drums and preached on street corners were often stoned, insulted and tossed into jail as disturbers of the peace.
>
> (from "Happy Birthday, Sally Ann!" by Dorothy Sangster, published in *Chatelaine*, June, 1982)

Exercise 6.1

Paragraph Order

Instructions:

1. Order the information in the following paragraph units.
2. State the kind of paragraph order you've used.

Problem 1

Purpose of paragraph: To inform about a laboratory class.

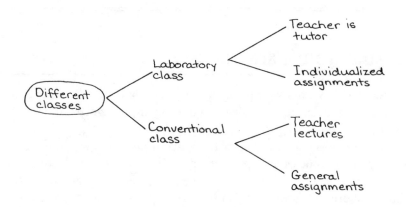

Problem 2

Purpose of paragraph: To tell someone how to make toast.

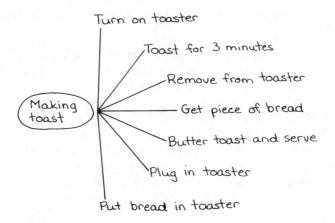

Problem 3

Purpose of paragraph: To explain the features of a new car.

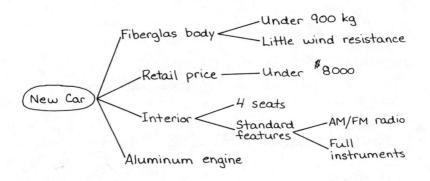

Ordering Your Paragraphs

Just as the details within your paragraphs demand order, so do paragraph units need to be arranged in a suitable order. Again, recognized orders of development often work for either the entire piece or sections within it. While you are working with your pattern, see if you can move the piece forward by using time order, space order, or an increasing or decreasing order of importance. See too, if parts can be ordered by a general to specific structure, a cause and effect order, comparison, or contrast.

Don't rely too heavily on these orders, however. Your job is to find the beginning in your pattern, then work the piece through the middle, to its end. Place your pattern in front of you and try different approaches. Look for obvious transition points. (Indicate these by drawing broken lines between connections.) Find an order that will hold your readers until you've finished what you have to say.

Here's an example of how a writer uses his pattern to build a pre-writing plan. The writer's statement of purpose is this:

> To inform the manager of the school cafeteria about the lineups and why they exist.

This statement of purpose leads to a control statement that answers the question *why*:

> Lineups are long and common in peak periods because not enough food is prepared beforehand and because the check-out system can't handle the volume.

The writer uses these statements, along with his observations, to build this pattern:

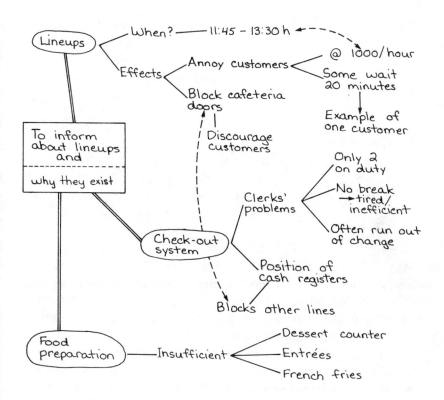

He decides that his pattern suggests four paragraph units. One paragraph will talk about the check-out system. Another will develop his contention that not enough food is prepared. A third paragraph will show how one customer waited for twenty minutes, and a fourth will develop the general problems with the long lineups.

A control statement that answers the question *why* sets up a cause and effect order. But, our writer still has decisions to make. Does he start with the causes and then develop the effect? And, in what order does he present the two causes? Anticipating his reader, he decides to order his report in this way; this is the writer's pre-writing plan:

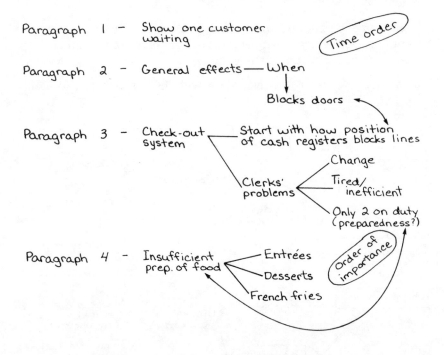

As you can see, pre-writing plans don't have to be neat. Some writers use arrows to indicate order; some number details right on their patterns. Other writers use scissors, cutting apart their patterns and arranging paragraph units like parts of a jigsaw puzzle. Some writers re-write their patterns as linear pre-writing plans.

Thus, although there is no set appearance, it is important to prepare a complete pre-writing plan. You should be able to look at your plan and know where you start and how to get to the end of your piece of writing.

The Process Continues

Use your pattern to order your writing assignment.

1. Determine your paragraph units. Each paragraph is controlled by a topic sentence.
2. Order the meaning in each paragraph unit. Use the basic paragraph orders as guides: time, space, order of importance, general to particular, cause and effect, comparison, contrast.
3. Order your paragraphs from the beginning to the end of your piece.

The final product of the pre-writing process is a pre-writing plan. It's like an architect's blueprint; it shows you where everything goes.

Final Assignment

Instructions:

Using the pattern you built for Final Assignment, Chapter 5, prepare a pre-writing plan.

Writing

7

Writing Your First Draft

The Writing Stage

Effective writing speaks to its readers. It is honest and real, never contrived or pretentious. Effective writers work at making their writing sound right. They begin by writing a successful first draft.

A successful first draft is a pre-writing plan in prose form—it has sentences and paragraphs. A successful first draft also leads the writer quickly into the re-writing stage of the writing process. This chapter explains how to write your first draft successfully. Its purposes are the following:

1. To emphasize the importance of an honest tone in your writing.
2. To explain when to use and how to write introductions and conclusions.
3. To give you some guidelines to follow when you are writing your first drafts.

Your Tone Decision

When you work from a pre-writing plan, writing a first draft is perhaps the easiest and shortest part of your writing process. All the pre-writing decisions have been made. Your task is simply to transform that plan into a piece of prose. Just string your information together in a manner that approaches the way you would speak to your readers. There's only one decision to make: what tone is most appropriate to your particular writing situation?

Every time you speak and write, it is within a certain context. You have something to say, and you have a purpose. That context has a bearing on the way you communicate. And, the way you communicate reflects your tone decision.

For example, the following words communicate the same meaning:

"Shut up!"
"O.K., quiet please."
"Hey, could you please keep it down out there?"

No one would use any one structure in all situations. In fact, I might use the first to try to get The Great Gatsby to stop barking, the second to begin a class, and the third to ask people in the hall to remember that a test is being written.

This use of different words structured in different ways is part of all speaking situations. And, even though you don't make a conscious decision about your tone, most of the time, the what, the why and the who of the situation direct you as you communicate. You speak differently to friends than to enemies, differently to people you know than to people you don't know, differently to those in authority than to those who are your peers. And, you speak differently according to what you are saying and why you are saying it.

Of course when you speak, you also use physical devices. Your tone of voice, facial expressions, body gestures and your use of silence are all part of your speaking tone. These physical devices, however, cannot be part of your writing tone. Consequently, the range of tones that you can establish as a writer is much more restricted than the range of tones you can use when speaking. But anytime you use prose structures, you are establishing a tone. It is partly your style—how you use words—and it is partly your attitude—how you decide to communicate in the writing situation.

Therefore, establishing a tone requires a decision—a decision, by the way, that every professional writer makes. Even publication systems have a policy about tone. Even though a newspaper or magazine employs many writers, the publication's attitude toward its readers is reflected in the tone of all the copy. Two of Toronto's morning newspapers illustrate different possibilities in tone. *The Globe and Mail*'s writers use a very objective tone; just the facts are given. Some people think that reading the *Globe* is like reading the statistics off a ticker tape. Here's a passage from an article:

> Consumers' Gas system has withdrawn a controversial proposal to revise its residential rate structure and has scaled down proposed rate increases to bring them into line with the federal Government's voluntary restraints program.
>
> The company told the Ontario Energy Board yesterday it "understands and agrees with" Ottawa's position on wage and price restraints and already is holding back salary increases for senior managers.
>
> "At the same time we feel it is important that the customers of Consumers' Gas are protected against undue inflationary influence," lawyer Stephen Paddon told the board as it opened hearings in Toronto into the rate proposals.
>
> (from *The Globe and Mail,* Toronto, August 4, 1982)

The Toronto Sun's writers, on the other hand, use a far more familiar tone. In fact, reading the *Sun* might be like listening to the person on the next bar stool. Here's the same news story as it appeared in the *Sun* on the same day:

> Consumers' Gas gave its 680,000 Ontario customers a break yesterday by adopting Ottawa's 6% solution.
>
> The gas company announced it will limit its request for a rate hike for its customers to 6% in line with the federal government's call for restraint.
>
> And the decision could signal a trend by other utilities and large industries to keep price hikes to within the 6% guideline, said Roy Phillips, executive director of the Canadian Manufacturers Association.
>
> (from *The Toronto Sun,* August 4, 1982)

The people who write for both newspapers understand their writing situation—why they are writing and to whom they are writing. Your tone decision is based on the same kind of understanding.

Writing Introductions and Conclusions

Introductions

Sometimes, you'll need to add an introductory paragraph that is not part of your pre-writing plan. This introduction is always written in the same tone as the body of your piece is written. Writing an introduction may be necessary for three reasons.

First, some forms of writing require an introduction. In an essay, for instance, manuscript guides call for a thesis statement presented in the introduction. A report or proposal requires an introduction, generally called a summary. It includes both the statement of purpose and the control statement, both written in the same tone as the body of the report or proposal. Business letters also have introductions. In a business letter, an effective introduction states why you are writing.

Second, you may decide that your first draft needs an introduction to make your purpose clearer. For example, here's a writer's statement of purpose:

> To persuade readers of the newspaper that smoking should be banned in public places.

He might decide that his article should be introduced with this opinion clearly stated. This introductory paragraph would be written in the same tone as the rest of the article.

Finally, introductions are written to interest readers. Writers have struggled with interesting introductions since "once upon a time". Four common methods that have been used (and perhaps overused) are these:

1. Ask a question. But, make sure that you answer it in the body of your piece.
2. Use a quotation.
3. Write an example. Show your readers a situation that leads into the body of your piece.
4. Startle your readers with an unknown fact.

Whether you use one of these introductions or another, an effective introduction is never an unnecessary part; it draws your readers into the body of your writing.

Conclusions

A conclusion is a paragraph (or paragraphs) that is added to the end of your writing. Deciding whether or not to write a conclusion and how to write it often depends on your decision about an introduction. Often, the reasons for writing a conclusion are the same as the reasons for writing an introduction.

Some writing forms demand a conclusion. A long essay (over 2,000 words) should have a conclusion that summarizes the main points in the paper. Likewise, proposals conclude with what should be done and how that task can be accomplished.

Sometimes, your decision about what to include in a conclusion relies directly on your decision about an introduction. For example, instead of stating his purpose in the introduction, the writer who wrote about banning smoking in public places might have concluded with his opinion. In such a case, he would have led his readers to this conclusion. Quite often, a modified statement of purpose can be used as either a conclusion or an introduction.

The common methods of writing conclusions are similar to those used when writing introductions. Attempting to wrap up their writing in an effective way, writers often add one of the following as a conclusion:

1. A question that is based on how the writer anticipates the response of the readers. For example, the writer who wrote about smoking in public might conclude with a question, such as:
   Do you want your children breathing others' cigarette smoke?
2. A quotation
3. An example.

Every effective conclusion ends a piece of writing in a satisfactory way; nothing new is added (nor is an apology made). A good conclusion, like an effective introduction, fits into the piece, not as an added-on part, but as the last important words you have to say.

The Process Continues

Writing your first draft can be the easiest and shortest stage of your writing process—if you work from your pre-writing plan, and if you write with the same flow of words you would use if you were talking to your readers. Remember, the first draft is not your final product. While writing your first draft, your task is simply to build your paragraph units with sentences. Try following these guidelines:

1. **Use your pre-writing plan.** Your pre-writing plan is the product of your pre-writing thinking; it maps out your first draft. You have built it for one purpose: to guide you as you write. Place it in front of you and get ready to write.
2. **Make your tone decision.** Try to imagine your reader sitting across the table. Write as you would talk.
3. **Write as quickly as you can.** There are two advantages to writing quickly. First, it helps you to establish your tone. Certainly when you speak, you don't stop and weigh every word. You speak with a flow of words. By creating that same kind of situation when you write, you are making your writing more real.
   The second advantage is this: the flow you develop will help you fill in meaning as you go along. Writing quickly won't solve all problems,

but often the flow you create will suggest additional ideas that should be included. If you are anticipating your readers effectively, you will automatically add details that you think are necessary.

Your flow of words, created by writing quickly, can improve the quality of your first draft. But a concern about spelling, grammar and punctuation at this stage can impede that flow. It is difficult to write quickly if you stop writing to check the spelling of a word or to ponder the use of a punctuation mark. Certainly these concerns are important, but they are not important while you are writing your first draft. By stopping and checking, and pondering and re-writing, you stop the flow and take yourself away from the reality of the writing situation. If you don't know how to spell a word, write something that looks similar. If you write a sentence that doesn't sound right, leave it. Continue writing. Remember, the process doesn't end until you have revised your first draft and written your second.

4. **Write on every third line of the page.** Many of the sentences you write will stand in your finished piece. But, some will need re-writing. By leaving room for your re-writing on the same page as your draft, you may save time.

5. **Write your introduction and conclusion last.** What you are writing may not require an introduction or conclusion. Read your finished draft and then decide whether you need these additional parts. If you decide to add either or both, write with the same flow and tone that you have established in the body of your writing.

6. **Write your first draft in one sitting.** Often this is impossible. But by leaving your first draft, you are interrupting your flow. Often, it is very difficult to pick up where you left off. So if your writing assignment is short enough to write in one sitting, make the time to do so. If it is a longer piece, break your writing at a major division in your pre-writing plan.

Final Assignment

Instructions:

Using the pre-writing plan you built for Final Assignment, Chapter 6, write a first draft. Follow the six guidelines presented at the end of the chapter.

8

Reviewing Your
First Draft

A Successful First Draft

Effective writing makes complete statements. Every sentence says something. Effective writers are very aware of the meaning of words and the
properties of a sentence. They make sure that their paragraphs are built
with clear words and complete sentences.

After writing your first draft, you need to check whether or not your
language is effective and your sentences are complete and doing their
jobs. This chapter examines three reviews of the writing stage of the
process. Its purposes are the following:

1. To show basic diction problems and how to solve them.
2. To show you what a complete sentence is and how to correct sentence
   fragments and run-on sentences.
3. To suggest how to review the effectiveness of your first draft.

Solving Diction Problems

When you read over your first draft, look for words which your readers
might not understand. Pay particular attention to specialized words, and
jargon and slang words. Let's look at specialized words first.

Specialized Words

Although occasionally specialized words present no meaning problem, most of the time such words don't communicate well. For instance, the word *balanoglossus* either means something to a reader or it does not. If that reader has studied advanced biology, perhaps it does. Otherwise, it may be just a series of letters.

Specialized words need to be defined. When you write a definition, you first tell your reader in what kind of classification the word falls, and then state how this particular thing differs from others in the same classification. For example, the word *balanoglossus* is defined first by stating what it is:

> A balanoglossus is a type of marine animal.

Of course, whales, walruses, and seals are also types of marine animals. Thus, you need to identify the word by defining it further. The complete definition for *balanoglossus* then becomes the following:

> A balanoglosus is a type of marine animal that is worm-like, soft-bodied, and has gill-like structures running the length of its body.

Deciding what words require definitions depends on who you anticipate your readers will be. If you think a word doesn't communicate well, define it.

Exercise 8.1*

Definitions

Instructions:

Write definitions for the five words given. Use a dictionary, but note that a dictionary does not always define explicitly by classifying and defining further.

1. meerschaum
2. ophthalmology
3. epistemology

4. navicular
5. platypus

Jargon and Slang

Jargon and slang words and expressions are shortcuts. When they are used between people who understand their meaning, effective communication is quite possible. However, much more often slang and jargon expressions are used which the readers do not understand. Try to guard against this situation.

Jargon words have a specific meaning associated with a particular study, occupation, hobby or sport. Here is a paragraph filled with the jargon of a particular sport:

> Yesterday I had a great thrill. While playing the *par-five* fourteenth, I scored a *double eagle*. My *drive* cleared the *dogleg* and settled in the *fairway* just beyond the *rough*. My second shot (I used a *five wood*) went over the *greenside bunker*, bounced on the front *fringe*, hit the *flag*, fell down the *pin* and settled in the *cup*.

The above example (with the jargon in italic) is about the game of golf. If you play golf, you understand the entire incident. If you don't, chances are you don't understand the event at all. The problem with jargon is that it relies on the writer and reader sharing a similar experience.

Many of your studies in school involve learning some jargon. Using these words when you communicate to your instructors and colleagues will probably not cause communication problems. But if you assume incorrectly that your reader understands your jargon, you will not communicate your meaning effectively.

Slang, like jargon, is restricted to a certain group of people, but it is usually limited further by time. Also, slang is less respectable than jargon. A group of high school students may share time together and start using expressions that have a specific meaning only for members of the group. Sometimes the expression can become popular across a continent. Examples might be *turkey* and *grass*.

However, slang words are too personal. They are constantly changing and can mean different things from city block to city block, from week to week. Like jargon words, slang words are acceptable in some kinds of writing, but their meaning is often too specialized. Therefore, unless your readers expect jargon and slang, avoid using them. Often, jargon words are best explained with a definition. Slang expressions can always be replaced with more understandable words.

Complete Sentences

Of course, all your words must be parts of complete sentences. Let's examine this basic unit of expression.

The Sentence — Two Requirements

A sentence has these two elements:

1. At least one subject/verb combination
2. At least one independent clause.

These two requirements are closely linked. The **subject** of your sentence is what you are communicating about. The subject's **verb** states what the subject is doing or what state it is in. To make a complete statement, this subject/verb combination must be in an **independent clause**.

Any one of your sentences can have more than one subject/verb combination, and more than one independent clause. But, no one sentence can neglect either of these two requirements. If it does, you've written a sentence **fragment**. A fragment does not communicate a complete idea. When finishing your first draft, you must examine your sentences and complete any fragments. This examination depends on your ability to recognize the subjects and verbs in your sentences.

Identifying Subject/Verb Combinations

Every sentence revolves around its verbs. Generally speaking, a verb is a word or a series of words used to express action. So in this sentence,

> Many girls *play* hockey.

the word *play* acts as the verb. A verb is also used to express a state of being. These verbs are called linking verbs. For example, in this sentence,

> She *was* a good player.

the word *was* acts as the verb. The words *is, are, was, were, has been, will be* and other forms of the verb *to be* are linking verbs. Other common linking verbs are *seems, appears, becomes,* and sense verbs such as *sounds, smells, tastes* and *looks*.

A verb can be more than a single word. Often, your verbs will consist of two or more words that state what your sentence's subject is doing. For instance, in this sentence,

> She *had been playing* hockey for ten years.

the words *had been playing* form the sentence's verb. And in this sentence,

> She *was stopped* from playing for the college team.

the words *was stopped* form the verb.

Problems arise when other action words are mistaken for a verb. Such words are called **verbals** and are classified as infinitives, gerunds and participles. Knowing these names is not important; however, thinking a verbal is a verb can mislead you as you check the completeness of your sentences. A verbal has one of three forms. A verb with the word *to* in front of it is an infinitive:

She was the first girl *to challenge* the courts.

The *ing* form of the verb is either a gerund or a present participle:

After *winning* in court, she quit the game.

Finally, the *ed* form of the verb (which is often formed differently with irregular verbs) is a past participle:

Exasperated by the proceedings, she took up boxing.

Verbals are often a part of a verb. That is, they act with other words to express action:

School officials *wanted to challenge* this woman who *was upsetting* the status quo, but they *were persuaded* by the school's lawyers to let the situation drop.

However, the infinitive (the *to* _____ form), and the present participle and gerund (the *ing* form) never act as a verb when they are alone.

Unfortunately, such a rule cannot be stated for the past participle. This form and the past tense of a verb are often the same word. Sometimes, it is difficult to determine how these words have been used. For example in the following sentences, the word *married* is used both as a verb and as a past participle:

She finally *married* another boxer on the team. Her husband, *married* to a fine sportswoman, expects to produce a family of athletes.

When in doubt about whether a word is a verb or a past participle, test the word by putting *which is, who is* or some form of this construction in front of the queried word. If the sentence makes sense with these added words, then the word is a past participle, not a verb. For example:

WHO IS

Her husband, **Λ** married to a fine sportswoman, expects to produce a family of athletes.

Thus, in this sentence the word *married* is not a verb, but a past participle.

Exercise 8.2 ＊

Identifying Verbs

Instructions:

Identify every verb in the following passage.

Steve Podborski grew up in the suburb of Don Mills on the outskirts of Toronto. Don Mills is the original Canadian suburb. Its curling streets are the model for the cookie-cutter pattern that has since been stamped out all across the country. He first skied on a nearby hill about 100 feet high. But from the age of 2½ to 14, he skied at Collingwood, two hours by car north of Toronto, on Blue Mountain, which at 600 feet is a mountain in name only. World Cup downhill courses fall through a minimum of 3,000 vertical feet...

The terrain of the Craigleith Ski Club at Collingwood was nevertheless appropriate for his first introduction to the techniques of downhill skiing. He and his brother played a game after each day's skiing: they would storm straight down from the top of the hill without turning. The idea was to gain enough speed to cover the long, flat stretch to their parents' chalet without having to walk or pole. That taught him sliding, an uncoachable skill that can earn vital microseconds on the long, high-speed flats of the World Cup downhills.

When Podborski was 9 the machinery of the highly organized Southern Ontario Ski Zone took over. He started racing in the Nancy Greene League, a series of interclub tourneys for the youngest racers, unique to southern Ontario at the time. At 13 he was competing in the Canadian Juvenile Championships in British Columbia. By 16 he had earned an invitation to the national team's annual fall selection camp. He was expected to admire the prowess of his elders but not to make the team. There were five downhills held at the camp. He won them all. "It was phenomenal," he recalls. "I couldn't believe it. Neither could they." He made the team.

(from "Fear of Flying" by John Barber, published in *Today*, January 30, 1982)

In a sentence, every verb has at least one subject. This subject and its verb are combined to form a subject/verb combination. (Sometimes a subject is left unwritten, and is "understood." For example, *you* is the subject of the sentence, *Sit down, please*.) The subject is connected to the verb; it is what or who is doing the action, or what or who is being. For example:

Many boys take ballet lessons.

In this sentence *many boys* is the subject. *Many boys* answers the question,

Who takes? Here's another example:

John was one such boy.

In this sentence, the subject is *John*. The word *John* answers the question, Who was?

But a subject does not have to be a specific person, place or thing. Often, words such as *it, who, which, that* and *this* act as a verb's subject. These words should refer back to a word in the same sentence or in an earlier sentence. For example:

He was a boy who hated the ridicule he got from his friends, but this did not stop him from loving ballet.

In the above sentence, *who* is the subject of the verb *hated*. The word *who* refers to *boy*, the word immediately before it. And, the word *this* acts as the subject of the verb *did not stop*.

As you've seen, any sentence can have more than one subject/verb combination. And, any single subject/verb combination can have more than one subject:

He and his father used to attend all the ballets in the area.

The verb *used to attend* has two subjects—*he* and *his father*. And, any single subject/verb combination can have two or more verbs:

He *studied* the techniques of the masters, *hoped* for a chance to prove himself, but never *practiced*.

When you are examining the subject/verb combinations in your sentences, you will notice these three common and correct constructions. First, you will find sentences where the subject is separated from its verb. In the following example, the subject *a master* is separated from its verb *saw*:

Finally one day, a master from one of the leading ballet companies in the country saw him dancing.

A group of words introduced by a preposition—words such as *of, from, in, between, against, with, on, up* and many more—often separates subjects and verbs. Prepositions are never verbs. They do not state action. Remember, a verb does not have to follow immediately after its subject.

Sometimes in fact, your sentence structure will reverse the usual order of subject followed by verb. In the following example, the second subject/verb combination in the first sentence is inverted; the subject *a difficult move* comes after the verb *was*:

In the middle of his audition was a difficult move. John fell; the master was not impressed.

Finally, note that the word *there* is not a subject. Usually when you use *there*, it is with a form of the verb *to be*. The subject follows the verb in this type of construction. In the first subject/verb combination of the following example, the subject *a moral* follows the verb *must be*. (Remember, the subject in this sentence answers the question, Who or what must be?)

There must be a moral to the story, but I don't know what it is.

Exercise 8.3 *

Identifying Subject/Verb Combinations

Instructions:

Identify every subject/verb combination in the passage used for Exercise 8.2. Remember that a subject/verb combination can have two or more subjects and two or more verbs.

Completing Fragments

The first requirement of a sentence is that it have at least one subject/verb combination. So if you have a structure that does not have a verb, this structure is a sentence fragment. And if you have a structure whose verb does not have a subject, then that too is a fragment.

These two kinds of fragments are easily fixed. To complete a fragment that does not have a verb, write a verb; give the subject some action. For those fragments that do not have a subject, the solution is even easier. Answer the question asked of your verb, and then write in the answer. For example, the following structure is a fragment because it does not have a subject:

Incorrect Have had interesting careers.

I can complete the fragment by writing in the answer to the question, Who have had interesting careers?

Shirley and Roger have had interesting careers.

Now this is a sentence.

Ensuring only that each structure has a subject/verb combination doesn't guarantee that it is a sentence. Many fragments have subject/verb combinations. These fragments are dependent or **subordinate clauses**. These clauses cannot stand alone; a subordinate clause is not a complete statement. For example, the following structure has a subject/verb combination:

Incorrect   Although they both studied at a drama school.

Yet, this structure is not a sentence; a subordinate clause depends on another statement to give it meaning. Thus, this kind of fragment can be completed by adding an **independent clause** to the subordinate clause:

Although they both studied at a drama school, *neither one is acting professionally.*

The independent clause is italicized. It is the main statement of the sentence and gives the subordinate clause meaning.

Subordinate clauses contain a subject/verb combination, but are introduced by either **subordinating conjunctions** (*although* is a subordinating conjunction) or **relative pronouns**. Both these kinds of words link a subordinate clause to an independent clause. In the following sentence, there are two subject/verb combinations but only one independent clause:

Shirley is a fashion designer who works in theatre productions.

Independent clause:

Shirley is a fashion designer

Subordinate clause:

who works in theatre productions

This subordinate clause is introduced by the relative pronoun *who*. The subordinate clause depends on the independent clause in the sentence to give it meaning.

Sometimes when writing a draft and in the heat of your work, you might write a subordinate clause instead of a sentence. When examining your sentences for completeness, look for this problem. There are three ways to fix it. You might have ended the sentence too soon as in the following example:

Incorrect   Because she has studied acting. The actors and actresses she works with respect her views.

If so, you can change your beginning and ending. Corrected, the sentence is written this way:

Because she has studied acting, the actors and actresses she works with respect her views.

Now the subordinate clause is linked to the independent clause within the same sentence.

Here's another situation. You might have written a subordinate clause that floats as an incomplete statement and is not linked to an independent clause anywhere in the piece:

Incorrect   While Roger teaches English at college.

There are two solutions to this kind of fragment. You can get rid of the subordinating word and make the clause an independent one:

Roger teaches English at college.

Or, you can add an independent clause to complete your statement. In the following example, an independent clause is added to the subordinate clause:

Shirley works days in the theatre while Roger teaches English at college.

*Exercise 8.4 ***

Completing Fragments

Instructions:

In the paragraph below, there are ten sentence fragments. Re-write the paragraph with complete sentences.

People in southern Ontario get very excited about snow-storms. They will tell you, for instance, about the "Blizzard of '78." How it was one of the worst storms in history. On January 26, the storm with howling winds that were recorded at over 170 km/h. Even though the radio stations had been warning drivers about the storm. Many drivers were caught unprepared. Were stranded on the roads all over the province. In one Service Center which is located on the MacDonald-Cartier Freeway west of London. Three hundred motorists were trapped for two days and a night. Others stayed in their cars. People who owned snowmobiles and four-wheel-drive trucks. Struggling through 3 m high snowdrifts, pushing stranded cars, rescuing motorists. In homes across the province, members of families waited. Some homes lost electricity and heat. In some communities, the hydro lines blown down in the 120 km/h winds. Before everything finally returned to a normal winter situation. Millions of dollars in property damage and many lives.

In the west, people don't become quite so hysterical about a little snowstorm.

Fixing Run-on Sentences

Every sentence has at least one independent clause. A sentence can also consist of an independent clause and one or more subordinate clauses. Finally, a sentence can contain two or more independent clauses, and each of these clauses can have subordinate clauses. For example, the following sentence has two independent clauses:

Roger teaches drama, and *he directs the school plays.*

The two independent clauses could be sentence units by themselves. They are connected within the same sentence by the coordinating conjunction *and.* (The most common coordinating conjunctions are *and, but, or, nor* and *yet.*) Another way to connect two or more sentence units within a single sentence is with a semicolon (;). The following sentence contains two independent clauses. Each one has a subordinate clause. A semicolon connects the two sentence units within the same sentence:

When he prepares for his classes, he uses the theory he learned in drama school; when he is directing, he uses the techniques he learned as an actor.

These two methods of joining independent clauses within a single sentence are the only acceptable ways. If you use a comma to connect two or more independent clauses, or if you simply write two or more independent clauses within a sentence, you are not building a correct sentence. These incorrect structures are called run-on sentences, or run-together sentences or fused sentences. A comma by itself cannot join two independent clauses within the same sentence. For example, the following structure is a run-on sentence:

Incorrect Roger has used his previous training, drama school has helped his career as a teacher.

If you find a run-on sentence in your draft, there are four solutions to the problem. You can make two sentences:

Roger has used his previous training. Drama school has helped his career as a teacher.

You can join the two independent clauses with the appropriate coordinating conjunction:

Roger has used his previous training, and drama school has helped his career as a teacher.

Because the ideas are closely related you can join the two independent clauses with a semicolon:

> Roger has used his previous training; drama school has helped his career as a teacher.

Finally, you can make one independent clause a subordinate clause by adding a subordinating conjunction:

> Because Roger has used his previous training, drama school has helped his career as a teacher.

Exercise 8.5 *

Fixing Run-on Sentences

Instructions:

Fix the run-on problems in the following sentences. Note that words such as *therefore, nevertheless* and *however* are not conjunctions.

1. Your sales are up, therefore, your bonus is forthcoming.
2. We sent your order #7320 to the Saskatoon store, the bill of lading is enclosed.
3. Her work is still inferior, nevertheless, she is improving.
4. This report analyzes our new fast foods division, it makes three recommendations.
5. While she was in Montréal, her secretary handled her correspondence.
6. The advertising campaign, launched on December 1, has had startling effects, sales are up 73% over last year.
7. I have consulted the legal division and am waiting for a decision.
8. The proposal was submitted on January 5, then, I waited for a decision.
9. The meeting was postponed no alternative date was set.
10. Your order for 15 gross of #27 fasteners arrived today, however, we are unsure about your shipping instructions.

The Process Continues

Most writers, no matter how experienced, cannot write a final copy from their pre-writing plans. Most review carefully before re-writing. They first examine and then re-structure their first draft. This reviewing stage follows the writing of a successful first draft. And what's success? Clear language and complete sentences that do the job. But, whether or not those sentences do the job effectively is sometimes difficult to judge. To help themselves, many writers leave some time between writing the first draft and examining it. Experience has taught them that a space of time allows them to be more objective about, or more critical of, their first draft.

Sue Grafton, who is a novelist, article writer, television script writer and screenplay writer, has written about writing a first draft and then "walking away":

> I go at it again and again and again until it's done. Fini. First draft at last. In the case of a novel, this process might take months, even years. For a short story, sometimes, blessedly, two days or even more. Whatever the time span, it is the easiest part of the cycle in some ways. It is hard work but it's exhilarating. My aim is to get it all out, not to let any one portion stand in my way. No writing of the first page over and over again. No getting hung up on chapter one. I move at a relentless pace, and when I reach the end, I sit back, panting. I stack up the papers on my desk; I walk away. I do errands, sit-ups, anything. I don't dare look at the piece. I can't stand to see it, I might go to a movie, read a book, call a friend, have a drink — anything to create distance between myself and my current torment...
>
> Eventually, I go back to page one and begin to read. I try to make my mind a blank, to look at the piece as though it were new and I were an objective, neutral observer taking it up for the first time.
>
> (From "The Creative Circle" by Sue Grafton, published in *The Writer,* December, 1977. Copyright© 1977 by The Writer, Inc.)

After your "backing off" period, your task is to finish your first draft. Read it, first of all, to check for fragments and run-on sentences. Read it also with your readers in mind. Be tough on yourself. Ask the following questions:

1. Have I communicated what I mean? Have I developed my ideas effectively?
2. Have I answered all the questions — what? when? where? how? to what degree? under what conditions? — that my readers need to know?
3. Have I defined or explained any words or expressions that my readers wouldn't know?
4. Is the meaning of each paragraph developed with ordered sentences?
5. Does the entire piece proceed logically from the beginning, through the body, to the end?

Work to answer *yes* to each question. Often, you will be able to make changes right on your draft. Sometimes, it may be necessary to re-write a part of your draft. Perhaps you will need to build a pattern for a part and then re-draft that part. Take whatever steps are necessary to make your first draft work. With a successful first draft, you can proceed to the re-writing stage of the writing process.

Final Assignment

Instructions:

Finish and submit the first draft you wrote for Final Assignment, Chapter 7.

Re-writing

9

Re-writing Your First Draft

The Re-writing Stage

Effective writing is built with correct and effective sentences. Unfortunately, completeness alone does not guarantee that a sentence is either correct or effective. For example, the following sentences, which were taken from letters received by a government department, are complete. They are not effective. Some complete sentences are nonsensical:

> In accordance with your instructions, I have given birth to twins in the enclosed cnvelope.

Some complete sentences are indirect and confusing:

> I am forwarding my marriage certificate and my three children, one of which is a mistake as you can see.

And sometimes, one incorrect word has disastrous (and hilarious) effects:

> Unless I get my husband's money soon, I will be forced to live an immortal life.

These examples of ineffective sentences show only a few of the kinds of problems you might face as you begin the re-writing stage of your process. No writer escapes this re-writing dilemma. A first draft, almost by definition, is full of sentences that can be made more effective. There they sit—sentences that are supposed to express your opinions and experiences. But, they don't quite do it. Perhaps the sound of the sentence is wrong. Perhaps the sentence doesn't seem to fit in its paragraph. Perhaps... So many different problems can confront you as you begin to re-write.

The next four chapters examine what to look for and how to re-write your sentences. This chapter starts by looking at the subject of each sentence. Its purposes are the following:

1. To explain what the focus and emphasis of a sentence are and how to identify them.
2. To show the major focus problems and how to re-write them.

Focus and Emphasis

Every sentence makes at least one statement about something or someone. That something or someone is the subject of the sentence's independent clause. This subject is called the **focus** of the sentence. The focus is what you are communicating about. The independent clause itself is the **emphasis** of the sentence. The emphasis is what the sentence is saying. The focus and emphasis are closely linked:

> **The emphasis of a sentence is the independent clause.**
> **The focus of a sentence is the subject (or subjects) of the independent clause.**

Thus, every complete sentence has a focus and emphasis. The question is, are they the most effective? Sometimes they are not. You need to examine each sentence's focus and emphasis and decide both of these questions:

1. Is the focus of the sentence what the sentence is really about?
2. Does the emphasis of the sentence make a clear and direct statement about the focus?

Exercise 9.1*

Identifying Focus and Emphasis

Instructions:

Identify the focus (or focuses) and emphasis (or emphases) in each of the following sentences.

1. Mary got home at 5:00 p.m.
2. Because he had to work late, Murray didn't get home until 7:00 p.m.

3. The ball game was over and the players were tired.
4. When the match was over, the team was exhausted.
5. Bill and his mother went to the movie.
6. As Eric couldn't go to the movie, his mother and sister went without him.
7. After the road went through the village, Moffat became much noisier and a place where no one wanted to live.
8. The policemen questioned the people who saw the accident.
9. Jim worked and saved his money, but when the price of the sports car was increased, he couldn't buy it.
10. Although the company faced a year that was predicted to be economically bad, the managers installed a computer.

Re-writing Weak Focuses

Meaningless-Focus Problems

Although many of the focuses in your draft sentences will be strong, others won't be. The first kind of weak focus to watch for is the meaningless one that uses words such as *it, that* and *this* when these words don't refer to anything specific. As a result, their sentences make statements about something unspecific or meaningless.

The **meaningless** *it* is the first meaningless-focus problem. Here are two sentences with the word *it* as focus:

> When Juan and Mary bought their new couch, it cost four hundred dollars. It is incredible that they got such a good deal.

In the first sentence, the *it* is meaningful, for *it* refers to *the couch*. The second sentence, however, has a meaningless *it* as its focus. The word *it* does not refer to a specific word.

There is nothing incorrect about a meaningless *it* if used appropriately. Often, statements about the weather use this construction:

> It is snowing in Newfoundland.
> It is raining in British Columbia.

However, the focus position is a strong one. By giving it to a meaningless word, you give up your chance to make a strong statement about something. In most cases, a meaningless *it* can be re-written, resulting in a more effective sentence.

The re-writing procedure for the meaningless *it* requires a close examination of your sentence; you must find a word or words that can replace the meaningless *it* as the focus of the sentence. In effect, you are asking yourself, what is this sentence really about? In the following example, although the focus is a meaningless *it*, the sentence is about buying good furniture:

Often it is impossible to buy good furniture at a reasonable price.

Once you have determined what the sentence is really about, substitute the new focus and make a statement about it. In this example, the re-write could be this:

Buying good furniture at a reasonable price is often impossible.

The meaningless *it* in the original sentence has been replaced by a stronger, more effective focus. The emphasis of the sentence has changed also.

Whenever you identify a meaningless *it* focus, you should follow this re-writing procedure. Sometimes, you may choose to leave the sentence as it is. But most often, this focus can be replaced with a more effective one. As a result, the sentence will become a more effective sentence. Here is another example that shows the re-writing procedure for meaningless *its*:

Sometimes, it gets very noisy in the library.

First, decide what the sentence is really about:

the noise in the library

Then make a statement about the new focus:

The noise in the library is uncontrollable sometimes.

The meaningless *it* is only one of two meaningless-focus problems. Often the second is more serious—the **meaningless** *this/that*. When these words are subjects and when they do not refer to a specific word, they are meaningless. Here's an example:

Often the heavy fog rises from the swamp. This makes driving difficult.

The *this* in the second sentence is a meaningless focus. Unlike the meaningless *it* which only weakens the focus position, the meaningless *this/that* can cause confusion because this problem affects the meaning of the sentence. In the above example for instance, the writer's meaning is unclear. *What* makes the driving difficult? Is it the fog rising from the swamp? Or is it the fog hiding the road? In any case, the writer has confused his readers by using a meaningless focus.

Every time you identify a meaningless *this/that* in your draft sentences, re-write the sentence. Follow the same procedure that is used for meaningless *its*. Here are some examples:

Yesterday Sam married Susie. This surprised everyone.

Re-write:

Yesterday Sam married Susie. This marriage surprised everyone.

Sometimes people in the library talk in loud voices. That makes studying difficult.

Re-write:

Sometimes people in the library talk in loud voices. The noise makes studying difficult.

February is the worst month, for the weather is cold and damp. This makes the winter too long.

Re-write:

February is the worst month. The cold, damp weather makes the winter too long.

Your solutions to meaningless-focus problems will change the emphasis of the sentence. This relationship between the focus and emphasis is constant. Once you change the focus, you have changed the emphasis. Thus, re-writing meaningless focuses can strengthen not only the focus, but also your emphasis.

*Exercise 9.2 ***

Re-writing Meaningless-Focus Problems

Instructions:

In the questions below, the words *it, this* and *that* are used as subjects. Some of them are meaningless focuses. Identify the meaningless focuses and re-write their sentences.

1. It isn't easy to find a good chocolate bar.
2. The test is on last term's work. This fooled me completely.
3. Please put the book on the empty shelf. It has a place there.
4. The football game was low-scoring. That was dull.
5. Anna broke off her engagement with John on the weekend. At times it seems as if they will never get married.

6. November is a long month and there are no holidays. This makes it seem even longer.
7. Fred went to work for his father. It seemed ridiculous that he should remain unemployed.
8. Scott asked if I had lied to him. This angered me.
9. It is apparent that Gina is brilliant.
10. It is not surprising that he took the job that pays the most money.

Misplaced-Focus Problems

Two other focus problems often creep into a writer's first draft. The first is the most easily recognized. The problem is characterized by personal pronouns—generally *I, we, one* or *you*—in the focus position. Certainly, these words can be strong focuses, but not if the paragraph or sentence is about something else. If, for instance, you are writing a description of a scene, and if you use the word *you* as the focus of a sentence, chances are you are using a misplaced focus. The following sentence is an example:

> Looking from the highway, you can see the lightposts of the football stadium rising over the rear of the campus.

This sentence is part of a descriptive paragraph. The focus is the word *you*. Clearly, this focus is misplaced, for the strong focus position has been given to a person who is not directly involved in the paragraph. The writer is not showing his readers what he sees, the real focus of the sentence—the lightposts of the football stadium.

Re-writing this kind of misplaced focus involves first of all eliminating all the words that refer to the misplaced focus. Just cross these words out of the sentence. In this example all words that describe the focus are crossed out. We are left with the following words:

> the lightposts of the football stadium rising over the rear of the campus

The next step is to find a verb that gives the new focus some action. In this example, the verbal *rising* easily becomes a verb. Here is the re-written sentence:

> The lightposts of the football stadium rise over the rear of the campus.

This new re-written sentence is more effective in the descriptive paragraph. It focuses on the lightposts and shows the readers the scene.

The same procedure can be used every time you discover a personal pronoun as a misplaced focus. Here are two additional examples of this re-writing procedure:

Leafing through the textbook, you can see that the author has used a great many illustrations.

Step 1: Eliminate all reference to the misplaced focus. These words remain:

that the author has used a great many illustrations

Step 2: Make a complete statement from the remaining words:

Throughout the textbook the author has used a great many illustrations.

Here's the other example:

Just before sunset we could hear the bats buzzing in the darkening sky.

Step 1: Eliminate all reference to the misplaced focus:

Just before sunset the bats buzzing in the darkening sky.

Step 2: Make a complete statement:

Just before sunset the bats buzzed in the darkening sky.

A word of caution about this kind of misplaced focus: in some situations, a person is the strongest, most effective focus. Sometimes re-writing may force you to a passive verb, which makes a weaker sentence overall. For example, the following sentence is the introductory sentence in a paragraph about the costs of skiing:

Before you start skiing, you should consider the costs.

Certainly this sentence can be re-written:

The expense of skiing should be considered before starting.

But, this re-written sentence implies the additional words *by someone*. In this situation, the original sentence is more effective. As the lead sentence, it attracts and speaks to its readers. Re-writing such a sentence does not make the paragraph more effective. And effectiveness — strong, clear expression — is what you are re-writing to achieve.

The last focus problem is not recognized so easily. The **buried focus** hides in the sentence; there is no sure way to detect it. Nevertheless, it is a misplaced-focus problem and, when re-written, can add power to your sentences and paragraphs.

Below are the first four sentences from a paragraph; the topic sentence is italicized:

Our new thumbtack is sure to outsell the competition. Painted with bright metallic colours, it features lightweight steel. The thumbtack's head has been enlarged for added convenience. Also, the thumbtack has a new electronically honed four-sided point that stays sharper longer.

Each sentence works to support the topic sentence. But, the fourth sentence demands further examination:

> Also, the thumbtack has a new electronically honed four-sided point that stays sharper longer.

The sentence's focus is *the thumbtack*. But, is this what the sentence is really about? The particular selling point in this sentence is *the point*. Yet this real focus is buried.

The re-writing procedure for this misplaced focus problem is quite similar to the one you use when re-writing meaningless *its*. First, decide what the sentence is really about:

> The new electronically honed four-sided point

Then, make a statement about that new focus:

> The new electronically honed four-sided point stays sharper longer.

This re-written sentence focuses on a major selling point of the thumbtack. The emphasis is stronger. Within the paragraph, the sentence is more effective.

Often when you examine your draft sentences, you will find a more effective focus buried in a sentence. Here are two more examples of this examination and re-writing procedure for the buried-focus problem:

> The festival attracts the best musicians, singers and dancers in the business.

Step 1: Determine what the sentence is really about:

> The best musicians, singers and dancers in the business

Step 2: Make a statement about the new focus:

> The best musicians, singers and dancers in the business come to the festival.

Here's the second example:

> The trees are full of squirrels scampering after food, playing with their mates and squawking at their human observers.

Step 1: Determine what the sentence is really about:

> Squirrels

Step 2: Make a statement about the new focus:

> Squirrels in the trees scamper after food, play with their mates, and squawk at their human observers.

In both of these examples, the writer has made a choice about a more effective focus and emphasis. Although the original sentences are neither wrong nor necessarily ineffective, the re-written sentences, in the opinion of the writer, do a better job. This decision is yours to make when you examine the focus and emphasis of your draft sentences.

Exercise 9.3 *
Re-writing Misplaced-Focus Problems

Instructions:

In each of the sentences below, the focus is misplaced. Re-write each sentence for a more effective focus and emphasis.

1. As dawn breaks, I can see the pine trees darkening against the sky.
2. The basket holds tiny toy soldiers carved from black walnut.
3. We could see an old potbellied stove just inside the door.
4. Right at the doorway, one can smell spaghetti with onions and garlic sauce.
5. Our new factory is equipped with the fastest, most complete conveyer system in North America.
6. At four o'clock, one can hear the closing bell, and the school yard is soon filled with children hurrying away.
7. Their living room walls are covered with expensive paintings.
8. Looking down the stream, you discover the fallen trees sinking into the water.
9. Just by walking into the warehouse, one can see that the foreman has paid little attention to the order of the merchandise.
10. One can see Niagara Falls from the observation deck of the CN Tower.

The Process Continues

Working through your first draft paragraph by paragraph, examine the focus of each sentence. Make sure it is what the sentence is really about. Watch for and re-write the three common focus problems:

1. meaningless *it*
2. meaningless *this/that*
3. misplaced focus, including buried focus.

Make sure that the emphasis of each sentence makes a strong, clear statement about its focus.

Review Assignment

Instructions:

The paragraph below is a successful first draft. However, it has several focus problems.

1. Identify the focus problems.
2. Re-write the paragraph with more effective focuses and emphases.

> The living room of the celebrity's house is very impressive. The southeast corner has a massive barn beam that supports and guards the entrance. In the southwest corner, you can see a tall pine corner cupboard. The stone fireplace which dominates the south wall is 3 m across and solid to the ceiling. Across the room, in the northeast corner, you discover a grand piano jutting into the room. There are four windows around the 8 by 10 m room. They start at waist level and climb to brass curtain rods suspended from the ceiling. Huge wall hangings, in burlap and heavy orange and red wools, hang on the walls between the windows. Three Canadiana antiques — an old kitchen cupboard, a Québec bedroom chest which is used as a liquor cabinet, and a settle bed — line the walls. This forces a feeling of space. The middle of the room is filled by a 3 m long highback couch in white corduroy. Between the fireplace and the couch sits a 3 m pine coffee table. Behind the couch you see an avocado tree climbing to the 4 m ceiling. This ceiling is stark white and untextured; this makes the room seem even larger. Natural colours and extremely good taste have been used in selecting the heavy wool shag rug that covers the entire floor.

10

Using Effective Subordination and Parallelism

Sentence Style

Effective writing has a mature style. Its sentences fill in the details, using the language correctly and effectively. Few sentences contain only the emphasis or independent clause. The effective writer adds specific details. Thus, the skeletal sentence

> The Tiger Cats beat the Blue Bombers.

becomes

> Last Friday evening, the Saint John Tiger Cats beat the Halifax Blue Bombers in a basketball game for charity.

These additional phrases and words develop the statement. They answer these questions: When did they play? Which Tiger Cats and Blue Bombers? Under what conditions did they play?

Such subordinate structures are the next re-writing targets. This chapter examines subordination and parallelism in the context of your re-writing process. Its purposes are the following:

1. To show the importance of subordination in strong statements.
2. To explain the functions and forms of standard subordinate structures.
3. To introduce the basics of correct and effective subordination.
4. To explain the importance and correct use of parallelism.

Avoiding Over-emphasis

Our use of subordination is taken for granted. Here's an example of what would happen without it. A writer has gathered information and is writing a description of a country kitchen. In the kitchen is an old black dog. The writer has decided to include four ideas about the dog. He writes these four sentences:

> The dog is old. The dog is black. The dog is sitting by the door. The dog is waiting for his master.

There are two problems with these sentences. First, the writing is immature and choppy; the tone is inappropriate unless the writer is writing to very young readers. Second, the writer has written four emphases; he has made all the ideas seem equally important. By emphasizing every experience of the dog, he emphasizes no experience.

The writer needs to make a decision. Let's suppose he is working with the idea of how old the kitchen is. His sentence about the dog should state that the dog is old. That idea would be the emphasis, and the other information would be subordinated:

> Even the black dog that waits for his master by the door is old.

Or, the writer might decide to emphasize that the dog is sitting by the door as part of a space order. The sentence might be written this way:

> Waiting for his master, an old black dog sits by the door.

The writer has other alternatives. But the decision should be based on which idea is the most important according to the topic. The remaining information is then subordinated into the sentence so that the writer does not emphasize too many ideas. You need to make the same decisions.

Functions of Subordinate Structures

Subordinate structures function as adjectives, adverbs, and occasionally as nouns. Each structure answers specific questions within its sentence.

When these structures add details about words or parts of a sentence, we say they **modify** the words or the parts of the sentence.

Adjectives

Adjectives modify a person, place, or thing; they either describe or qualify. If an adjective describes, it answers the questions *what?* or *what kind of?* , as in this example:

He attended a *wild* party.

If an adjective qualifies, it answers the question *how many?* or *how much?*

He knew *three* people.

Adverbs

Adverbs modify a verb, an adjective or another adverb. Adverbs answer most of the questions related to subordinate structures. They answer *where?*

The party was *at his parents' house.*

They answer *when?*

It was held *when his mother and father thought the kids were away.*

Adverb subordination answers the question *how?*

John heard about the party *by asking a friend.*

And *to what degree?*

The friend told him it would be *very* difficult to get an invitation.

It answers the question *under what conditions?*

He decided to go *if he could find a disguise.*

And *why?*

He left the party *because he couldn't believe what he saw.*

Nouns

Nouns are words which name persons, places, or things. Generally, they are the focus and the completion of an emphasis, but nouns are used occasionally as subordinate structures. Noun structures answer the question *what?*

He knew *that he could never tell anyone.*

In some constructions, they answer the prompting question *that is . . . ?* or *who is . . . ?*

He didn't even tell Susan, *his girlfriend.*

Forms of Subordinate Structures

The examples above show that subordinate structures take various forms. Sometimes they are clauses; a subordinate clause always has a subject/verb combination. Or, they are phrases; although there are several kinds of phrases, a phrase never has a subject/verb combination. Or, they are word groupings.

Clauses

As you know, subordinate clauses have a subject/verb combination, but cannot stand alone; they need an independent clause, or emphasis, to give them meaning. All three kinds of subordinate clauses—noun, adjective and adverb—answer specific questions within their sentences.

Noun clauses have two forms. Either they begin with a subordinating conjunction (usually *when, where, how* or *why*), or they begin with a relative pronoun (usually *that, who, whoever, what* or *whatever*):

One day his father asked him *where he had been that evening.*
John told him *what he wanted to know.*

Adverb clauses always begin with a subordinating conjunction. The most common subordinating conjunctions are the following:

after, although, because, before, if, since, unless, when, whenever, where, wherever, whether, while

Here's an example of an adverb clause:

John and his father decided not to tell his mother *because she would get upset.*

Adjective clauses have two forms. In both forms, the clause starts with a relative pronoun; the most common relative pronouns are the following:

that, when, where, which, who, whom, whose

In the first form of adjective clause, the subject of the clause follows the relative pronoun:

Sheila met a man at the party *whose hometown is Nanaimo, B.C.*

The second form of adjective clause also begins with a relative pronoun. However, the relative pronoun itself is the subject of the clause:

She goes out with another guy *who lives in Corner Brook, Newfoundland.*

Phrases

Phrases are either prepositional or verbal. **Prepositional phrases** are the easiest to recognize. They begin with a preposition and are followed by a noun that may or may not be modified. The nine most common prepositions are the following:

at, by, for, from, in, of, on, to, with

Prepositional phrases function as either adjectives or adverbs. As an adjective, they answer the question, *what?*

All *of Sheila's boyfriends* live away from her hometown.

All *what?* All of Sheila's boyfriends. Here's another example:

Letters *from her boyfriends* arrive every day.

What letters? Letters from her boyfriends.

And as adverbs, they answer all the adverbial questions. In the following example, the prepositional phrase answers the question, *where?*

She met the naturalist *on Baffin Island.*

Verbal phrases come in various forms and have different functions. They are either participle phrases or infinitive phrases. The participle phrase has two forms, but only one function. The infinitive phrase, in contrast, has only one form, but can serve three functions.

Participle phrases are always adjectives, even though they suggest action. There are present participle phrases and past participle phrases. The present participle phrase begins with an *ing* word, the present participle, and is followed by words related to that action. For example:

One day, she saw a group of musk oxen *trudging along the northern tundra.*

Past participle phrases are constructed the same way, but the *ed* form of a verb, the past participle, is the first word in the phrase. (Some past participles are irregular; more about that in Chapter 12.) Here's an example of a past participle phrase:

Blinded by the sun, one musk ox wandered away from the herd.

Infinitive phrases always begin with the word *to*. The next word is an action word. These two words form the infinitive of a verb. The remaining words in the phrase relate to the action expressed by the infinitive. An infinitive phrase can serve as an adjective:

She found a way *to direct the stray back* to the herd.

An infinitive phrase can be an adverb:

To show his appreciation, her new friend, the naturalist, took her to Newfoundland for the weekend.

And, an infinitive phrase can function as a noun:

She wanted *to stay away* from Corner Brook.

Words and Word Groupings

Words and word groupings are also subordinate structures. **Adjectives**, as you know, modify a noun or pronoun:

They took a *slow* boat to Newfoundland.

Adverbs modify verbs, adjectives and other adverbs. Often, the adverb is the *ly* form of the adjective:

She got off the boat *slowly*.

Noun subordinate structures are the appositive, the gerund or the gerund phrase. An appositive gives more information about another noun. It answers the question *that is?* or *who is?*

The boat, *The Canadian Temptress*, took three days to make the journey.

The gerund is an *ing* word that serves as a noun. For example, in the following sentence the *ing* word is clearly a thing. (Don't forget, when an *ing* word acts as an adjective, it is a participle.) In this sentence, *fighting* is a gerund:

Her boyfriend from Edmonton loves *fighting*.

A gerund phrase also serves as a noun:

He likes *fighting Sheila's other boyfriends*.

Here's a review of the functions and forms of basic subordinate structures:

FUNCTIONS

FORMS	Adjective	Adverb	Noun
Clauses	r.p. + s/v comb r.p. + v	s.c. + s/v comb	r.p. + s/v comb s.c. + s/v comb
Phrases	prepositional participle present past infinitive	prepositional infinitive	 infinitive gerund
Words and Word Groupings	adjectives	adverbs	 appositive gerunds

Note: r.p. = relative pronoun
s.c. = subordinating conjunction
s/v comb = subject/verb combination

*Exercise 10.1**

Identifying Subordinate Structures

Instructions:

Identify both the function and the form of the italicized structures in the following sentences.

Example:

When you do this exercise, use the previous pages as a reference.

Answer:

Adverb clause *or* Function—Adverb; Form—Clause

1. He knows *that you are coming*.
2. She bought the puppy *that sat in the store window*.
3. The boy *with the football* is very good.
4. That *short, fat* guy is her husband.
5. *Speeding on gravel roads* is dangerous.
6. *Barking with excitement*, the dogs ran across the lawn.

7. They climbed Mount Fairweather, *the highest mountain* in British Columbia.
8. Those students are assured jobs, *provided they can complete the training program*.
9. I was *very* glad to see him.
10. They were afraid *to drive through the mountains*.
11. The course *taught at college* is interesting.
12. I found the ring *behind the house*.
13. He left the room *quietly*.
14. That teacher, *whom I respect as a hockey coach*, is boring in class.
15. They borrowed money *to help them* through the setback.

Correct Subordination

Three major subordination mistakes cause incorrect and confusing sentences:

1. Incorrect form
2. Misplaced subordinate structures
3. Dangling subordinate structures.

Incorrect Form

Using the wrong form of subordination occurs most often when you use an adjective form to answer an adverb question. This error occurs most often with single words. Here's an example:

Incorrect When George heard that Sheila was in Newfoundland, he flew there quick.

Clearly, the word *quick* answers the question *how did he fly?* It should therefore be in the adverb form *quickly*. Sometimes, clauses will take the wrong form as well. For example, the following adverb clause is incorrectly introduced by a relative pronoun:

Incorrect He went to the hotel which she was staying.

You should always check your subordinate structures to make sure they are complete and formed correctly.

Misplaced Subordinate Structures

Subordinate structures, when misplaced, can severely alter the meaning of a sentence. For example:

> *Incorrect* Wearing a new dress, George found her in the hotel bar.

Obviously, George wasn't wearing the new dress; Sheila was. But, the way the sentence has been written puts him into the dress.

Misplacing subordinate structures occurs most often with adjective subordination. Adjective subordinate structures must be placed directly before or after the noun or pronoun they modify. So, let's put the dress on Sheila:

> He found her wearing a new dress in the hotel bar.

Now the participle phrase *wearing a new dress* follows directly after *her*, the pronoun it modifies. Always check subordination and make sure it is placed where it should be.

Dangling Subordinate Structures

Using dangling subordinate structures is as serious a mistake as misplacing subordinate structures. Sometimes, the result can be even more ridiculous. For example:

> *Incorrect* Seeing her with another man, his stomach felt as if it had been kicked.

This sentence states that his stomach saw her with another man, for the adjective participle phrase, *seeing her with another man*, is positioned before *his stomach*. A dangling subordinate structure stands alone; there is nothing in the sentence which the structure directly modifies. This sentence has no *George* or pronoun substitute; the phrase just dangles without anything to talk about. Most often, this problem occurs with adjective participle phrases. You can fix such a mistake in two ways. First, you can make the phrase an adverb clause:

> When he saw her with another man, his stomach felt as if it had been kicked.

Or second, you can change the independent clause so that the phrase doesn't dangle:

> Seeing her with another man, he felt a knot in his stomach.

Now the adjective participle phrase modifies the pronoun *he*.

Effective Subordination

Fixing the three mistakes described above will make your sentences correct, but not necessarily effective. Here are four additional objectives you should strive to achieve.

1. **Variety.** Try to vary the kind of subordinate structures you are using. Most of us use the structures we are most comfortable with, the ones that just roll off the pen. Normally these are fine, but every writer should check to make sure that sentences have some variety. Perhaps a clause can be replaced with a stronger participle phrase. For example, the following sentence has a clause:

    She last saw him as he was leaving for home.

    But for variety, the writer might re-write, using a participle phrase:

    She last saw him boarding the airplane.

2. **Specifics.** Make sure that your subordinate structures are specific. Answering questions with vague generalizations wastes words. For example, here's a common construction:

    We will ship your order soon.

    The word *soon* answers the question *when?* But, can you say exactly when *soon* is? If you are going to answer questions, be specific. Even the following sentence is better; the adverb subordinate structure is doing its job:

    We will ship your order when it is completed.

3. **Brevity.** Avoid wordiness in your subordinate structures. A good rule is to use the shortest construction that specifically says what you want to say. So, use a word rather than a phrase, and a phrase rather than a clause. Here is a draft sentence and its re-write:

    He left when the sun came up.

    Re-write:

    He left at dawn.

4. **Simplicity.** Guard against piling subordination on subordination. Here's an example of the kind of sentence you should try to avoid:

    When he left, he took a plane which flew to St. John's, which is Newfoundland's capital, established in the sixteenth century.

    There is nothing absolutely wrong with the sentence, but one clause describes the plane, another describes St. John's, and then a phrase describes the capital. By the end of the sentence, the reader has lost any sense of the sentence's emphasis.

In business writing, some consultants suggest that a sentence should have only one final subordinate structure. The preceding sentence would become two sentences:

> When he left, he took a plane to St. John's. The city was established in the sixteenth century and is Newfoundland's capital.

Exercise 10.2*

Fixing Incorrect and Ineffective Subordination

Instructions:

Each of the sentences below has a subordination problem. Re-write each sentence to make it either correct or more effective.

1. Running with his tail between his legs, Jim saw the dog.
2. The biggest facility in the world, he arrived at the new airport.
3. Dressed in a rented tuxedo, Mary took Bob to the formal.
4. He did excellent on his exams.
5. During the evening, he almost drank fifteen cups of coffee.
6. Our new car arrived at the dealership loaded down with extra equipment.
7. When served with butter and maple syrup, everyone enjoys pancakes.
8. Before stopping for a rest, the bench looked inviting.
9. The company is sending the package soon.
10. This recipe can be prepared quickly.
11. He was moderate skilled in fishing.
12. While waiting in line for the concert tickets, the rain stopped.
13. After watching the sunset, a walk looked inviting to me.
14. The Festival of Friends is annually held in Hamilton which is the largest outside free music event in Canada.
15. They thought about taking a trip around the world for a day, but chose not to.
16. Ellen watched the thunderstorm doing her homework.
17. In the month of November, everyone in Canada is in a bad mood.
18. They carried her to her place of residence in an inebriated condition.
19. The car circled around the house and then disappeared from view.
20. He is a person who can be depended upon to do what he says he will do.

Parallelism

As you've seen, an important re-writing task is making the most important idea the emphasis of the sentence and subordinating other details. Sometimes, however, two or more ideas in a sentence are equally important; both should remain independent clauses. There are two effective ways to make two ideas parallel.

Coordinating Conjunctions

When a sentence has two or more independent clauses, a coordinating conjunction connects them. This coordinating word (the most common are *and, or, but, for* and *yet*) indicates that what comes before it and after it are equal in value. For example:

> Warren went to buy the steak, *and* Joanne went to purchase the wine.

The coordinating conjunction *and* connects the two equal independent clauses, the emphases of the sentence.

Correlative Conjunctions

Correlative conjunctions also connect equal ideas. These words come in pairs, and the most common are these:

> either/or, neither/nor, not only/but also, both/and

When you use a pair of correlative conjunctions to join emphases, the first word of the pair introduces the first emphasis, and the second word of the pair introduces the second emphasis. Any of the independent clauses can have modifiers. For example:

> *Either* they both help to prepare their meals, *or* they decide to dine out.

The sentence has two emphases connected by the correlative conjunctions *either/or*.

The principle of parallelism is just this simple: a construction that is written on one side of a coordinating word must be equal in function and form to the construction on the other side of the coordinating word. Thus, if you are writing two emphases in a sentence, there are two correct sentence models:

	coordinating	
(Emphasis)	conjunction	*(Emphasis)*

correlative		correlative	
conjunction	*(Emphasis)*	conjunction	*(Emphasis)*

Parallelism in Subordinate Structures

This same principle applies to subordination. Whenever you join two or more subordinate structures with a coordinating word, those structures must have the same function and form. Thus, the following sentence is incorrect:

Incorrect   The steak was big, juicy and an expensive item.

The adjectives *big* and *juicy* are positioned as if they were equal to the noun *item*. Instead, the sentence should read this way:

The steak was big, juicy and expensive.

Now, the function of the three subordinate structures is the same; all are adjectives.

Not only must subordination be parallel in function, but also it must be parallel in form. A clause cannot be equal to a phrase. For this reason, the following sentence is incorrect:

Incorrect   Joanne bought a bottle of wine from the Okanagan Valley and that competes with more expensive French wines.

The phrase *from the Okanagan Valley* cannot be equal to the clause *that competes with more expensive French wines.* Either both structures should be phrases or both should be clauses. Here's a possible re-write:

Joanne bought a bottle of wine that was produced in the Okanagan Valley and that competes with more expensive French wines.

Also, the phrases that surround the coordinating word must be the same kind. For instance, an infinitive phrase and a gerund phrase are not equal:

Incorrect   They both like to eat good, rare steak and drinking fine but inexpensive wine.

Each must be an infinitive phrase:

They both like to eat good, rare steak and to drink fine but inexpensive wine.

Or, each must be a gerund phrase:

They both like eating good, rare steak and drinking fine but inexpensive wine.

Correlative conjunctions join equal subordination as well. When using these pairings, make sure that the same construction follows both the first and the second word in the pairing. Here's an incorrect use of correlatives:

> *Incorrect*   Not only do they like to drink the wine but also buying it.

This is a possible re-write of the sentence:

> They like not only to drink the wine but also to buy it.

*Exercise 10.3 ***

Parallelism

Instructions:

In all but one of the following sentences, there is at least one parallelism problem. Identify the problems and re-write the sentences without changing the meaning.

1. To serve and protecting are the policeman's responsibilities.
2. The house with the indoor swimming pool and that overlooks the Pacific Ocean is for sale.
3. A sporting goods company has just announced the development of an indestructible and cheaply hockey stick.
4. Situated in the middle of the room and with a throw-rug sits a white corduroy couch.
5. The house was sold quickly and without problems.
6. He found the treasure either by deducing the route to the cache or because he tortured the only man who knew the location.
7. The student who won the design award and who was offered the scholarship has been hired to teach first year students next year.
8. If the book is not published, either the decision was made because the story is unsaleable or because the author is unknown.
9. She dreams of neither material goods nor being a famous person.
10. The room was not only large, but also it was unfurnished.

The Process Continues

After you have sharpened the focus of your sentences, the next step is to examine the emphasis and the subordinate structures of each sentence. What idea (or ideas) you choose to make the emphasis of the sentence and what ideas you choose to subordinate depend on what you are writing about and your purpose. When revising and re-writing for correct and effective emphasis and subordination, keep these tips in mind:

1. Avoid over-emphasis.
2. Use the correct form to answer the question you are answering in the subordination.
3. Position your subordinate structures correctly.
4. Avoid any dangling subordination.
5. Vary the kind of subordinate structures you use.
6. Use specific words in your subordinate structures.
7. Avoid wordiness; use the least number of words possible to say what you mean.
8. Avoid piling subordination on subordination, especially at the end of a sentence.
9. Use parallelism to show the equality of subordinate structures and of emphases.

Review Assignment

Instructions:

In each question below, one sentence is italicized. That sentence is the emphasis of the new sentence you are to write. This new sentence will include, as subordinated parts, the other sentences in the question.

Example:

Sarah left work early.
She felt sick.

Possible Answer:

Because she felt sick, Sarah left work early.

Note:

In most questions, there is no single correct answer. Write your sentences with correct and effective subordination and, where applicable, correct parallelism. There are many possible *incorrect* answers.

1. *A highback couch fills the middle of the room.* The couch faces the fireplace.
2. *The dog is a Great Dane.* The dog is big. The dog is black.
3. *The prisoner escaped.* There was a tunnel under the cell.
4. *Susan had a baby.* It was a boy. He weighed 2.4 kg when he was born.

5. *The desk sits in the corner of the room.* The desk features brass hardware.
6. *My friend called the fire station.* His house was on fire.
7. Brian is a poor dancer. His wife wants to go dancing. *Brian is going to take dancing lessons.*
8. *Going to university will be difficult for him.* His marks are not very good.
9. *That apartment building is full.* It just opened last month.
10. *The house was built last year.* The house needs many repairs.
11. *I saw him yesterday.* He was walking across the bridge.
12. *I'm playing golf with Henry.* Henry is my neighbour. He doesn't play very well.
13. *Monika just left the house.* She was driving her new car.
14. Art ran the race. *Art finished last.* He ran poorly.
15. *She likes her summer job.* She plants trees.
16. *Mr. Smith likes to study and organize on Saturday mornings.* He studies the weekly stock market quotations. He likes organizing his investment plans for the following week.
17. George has a full-time job. George is an A-average student. *George is planning to get married.*
18. *Above all else, she likes two things.* She likes a good car. She likes having money.
19. *He bought the car.* It was the one in the showroom window. It was owned by a famous politician.
20. *This assignment tests two things.* It tests your use of effective subordination. It tests how you handle parallel structure.

11

Re-writing for
Verb Power

Strong Verbs

Effective writing has power and force. Effective writers work to make each sentence contribute to this power. Where do they begin? They look at the verbs in each sentence, for while the focus of a sentence is the center, the verbs give a sentence energy. Verbs are the points of power and strength in a sentence.

Yet many writers, by using weak verbs, lessen the effectiveness of their writing. In some sentences, the subjects just exist:

Her book *is* about the history of Canada.

Some verbs waste the potential of an effective position:

The country's development *can be seen* through the pages.

Sometimes, a long verb combination delays the action:

But, the public *hasn't paid any attention* to the book.

And, some verbs are simply weak and lifeless:

It *stays* on the discount shelf in bookstores.

The verbs of such sentences demand examination and re-writing. These sentences can be improved considerably:

Her book *describes* the history of Canada. Through the pages, the country *grows*. But, the public *has ignored* the book. It *gathers* dust on discount shelves.

This chapter examines the re-writing of weak verbs. Its purposes are the following:

1. To show the importance of strong, active verbs.
2. To give a checklist of what to examine when revising the verbs in your draft sentences.
3. To explain how to re-write ineffective verbs and how to use a dictionary of synonyms as a resource.

Examining Your Verbs

To this point in the writing process, verbs have certainly been necessary. However, they have received little attention. Like the basting used by a dress designer, they have served their purpose. But, now that your sentences have the shape and form you want, it's time to put in the strong, holding stitches. It's time first to examine and then, if necessary, to re-write your verbs.

There are five verb constructions you should examine. Not every one necessarily demands re-writing, but you should consider the alternatives you have to the following verb constructions.

Long Verb Combinations

These structures delay the action of the verb. They crawl like a five-yard-a-play movement down a football field. There is none of the excitement of a long kick-off return. Yet, a good verb will give a sentence the necessary rush. Here's an example of this weak kind of construction:

Helen walks with a limp.

Since she doesn't limp when she lies down or sits at her desk, write the sentence this way, instead:

Helen limps.

Sometimes, the negative delays the action of the verb. A statement such as

He cannot remember the date of his anniversary.

is generally stated better this way:

He has forgotten the date of his anniversary.

Often, weak constructions use adjective or adverb subordination to do what a verb can do with fewer words and more impact. Look at this sentence, for example:

> Ted spoke loudly and unkindly to his sister.

It might be re-written this way:

> Ted screamed at his sister.

And sometimes, trendy constructions are used; the media often pick up expressions such as this one:

> They made their escape from Iran.

Even if you want to be a media star, re-write the sentence this way:

> They escaped from Iran.

Exercise 11.1*

Re-writing Long Verb Combinations

Instructions:

Each of the sentences below can be re-written with a shorter verb that has more impact. Revise and re-write each sentence.

1. Susan cannot remember the date of her graduation.
2. Last night at Leslie's party, Eva did not pay any attention to me.
3. His speech was full of long, windy phrasing and superfluous material.
4. The reason he left school was that his money was running short.
5. He moved toward the door on the tip of his toes.
6. Stephen did not have much confidence in his partner's honesty.
7. Sharon was the recipient of the new scholarship.
8. The two lovers talked in soft voices in the corner of the café.
9. Ernie sat with a slovenly posture.
10. At the meeting, Catherine read her report about the conditions on the reserve.

Passive Verbs

Passive verbs are generally weaker than active verbs. What is the difference? When a verb is in the active voice, its subject is doing something. When a verb is in the passive voice, however, its subject is having something done to it. Consider this sentence:

> Wilda is carrying the canoe.

The subject, Wilda, is doing something. What she is doing—described by the verb *is carrying*—is active. But the next sentence is formed differently:

> The canoe is being carried by Wilda.

Here, the subject, the canoe, isn't doing anything. In fact, it's being done to. The verb—*is being carried*—is in the passive voice.

When reviewing for passive verbs, remember that sentences that have passive verbs often have a *by someone* or *by something* construction. Even if the phrase isn't written, it is implied. For example:

> The boat was pulled onto the beach. (by someone)

Because an active verb is shorter and expresses action, it is preferred over a passive verb.

Exercise 11.2 *

Changing Passive Verbs to the Active Voice

Instructions:

The verbs in some of the sentences below are in the passive voice. Determine which sentences are written with passive verbs and re-write those sentences so that the verbs are active. You may have to create a subject to do the action.

1. Part-time jobs are taken by many students.
2. All the candles on the cake were blown out.
3. The filing system has been redesigned.
4. McClelland and Stewart are publishing that book next spring.
5. The new book is being edited by Mrs. Grady.
6. The private member's bill was defeated by parliament.
7. Douglas will have completed his assignment by Christmas.
8. Because of the mail strike, the contract is being delivered by courier.
9. By the time I got to the store, all the specials were sold out.
10. The scoring record was set by Wayne Gretzky.

Sense Verbs in the Passive Voice

These kinds of verbs sometimes creep into your draft sentences. Often, they are ineffective. Here's an example:

> Frigid air *can be felt* from Lake Athabasca.

The passive verb *can be felt* wastes the verb's potential. It implies the phrase *by the writer*, yet the writer has nothing to do with the content of the sentence. Also, this weak verb tells us nothing about what that frigid air is doing.

There is/There are Constructions

These weak verb constructions result in the same problem caused by sense verbs in the passive voice. They don't make anything happen, and instead, tell us only that their subjects *are*. *There is/there are* constructions, also called **expletive** constructions, use the word *there* followed by a form of the verb *to be*. We all use this construction too often, as in the following sentence:

There were two bad storms last winter.

In the expletive construction, the subject follows the verb. In the above example, the subject is *two bad storms*, and the sentence doesn't tell us what those storms did. Perhaps they closed schools, blocked highways or sank ships. But, we only know that they *were*.

The Verb *To Be*

The expletive isn't the only construction that uses the verb *to be*. This verb, in all its forms, is continually expressing what *is* or *are, were* or *was*; it expresses a state of being rather than an action. For example:

The weatherman is on at 6:40 p.m.

But, what does the weatherman do?

The verbs in a sentence convey action. Finding the verb that expresses that action with the most power is the re-writing task. When each verb is powerful, each sentence is more effective; the composition has a punch that it didn't have before. The power of the verbs makes an impact on your entire piece.

Re-writing Your Verbs

When you re-write your verbs, make the subjects in your sentences do something. That action should be specific and dynamic, never delayed by subordination, negatives or worn-out expressions.

Re-writing long verb combinations and weak passive constructions demands recognizing the problem and then doing something about it. Replacing passive sense verbs, the expletive and the verb *to be* often requires some extra hard thinking. The task forces you to go into your store of words and pull out the right verb, the one that states exactly what your subject is doing. Often, this job is frustrating. You've worked with that sentence for a while; the words stare back at you, challenging your vocabulary. Fortunately, writers have an invaluable aid — a dictionary of synonyms. This resource lists words alphabetically. Words with similar meanings are presented with each entry. Here's an example entry from *The New Roget's Thesaurus*:

> **act,** *v.* function, operate, work, take steps, put into practice (ACTION); play, act out, present, enact, take the part of (ACTOR); behave, acquit oneself, conduct oneself (BEHAVIOR); pretend to be, impersonate, pose as (PRETENSE); officiate, officialize, execute (OFFICIAL).

A dictionary of synonyms is a memory refresher. Not all the words listed are the right words. In fact, most are probably inappropriate for any given sentence. So, never use a dictionary of synonyms to find a new, impressive sounding word. Use it instead to remind you of words you already know. That reminder should help you search for the right action word.

With your dictionary of synonyms beside you and your weak verb constructions identified, you can begin to put some punch into your draft sentences. Here's the re-write procedure for passive sense verbs. First, cross out the verb along with any construction in the sentence that refers to it. For example:

> An old black dog can be seen resting by the back door.

The structure becomes this:

> An old black dog resting by the back door

Then, make a sentence by stating what the subject is doing. In this sentence, the *ing* word *resting* easily becomes the verb of the sentence:

> An old black dog rests by the back door.

Sometimes however, the original sentence doesn't offer a new verb. Here's an example:

> Frigid air can be felt from Lake Athabasca.

When the passive verb is eliminated, we have these words remaining:

> Frigid air from Lake Athabasca

Now, the task is to give that frigid air some action. Ask yourself, what does it do? Well, it *blows*. Put the verb *blows* in the sentence:

Frigid air blows from Lake Athabasca.

If *blows* isn't the right verb, go to your dictionary of synonyms and find the right word, the verb that expresses your statement about the frigid air.

Exercise 11.3 *

Re-writing Passive Sense Verbs

Instructions:

Re-write the sentences below with strong, active verbs. Use a dictionary of synonyms if you need a memory refresher.

1. Fifteen minutes before closing time, that employee can be seen leaving the factory.
2. Squirrels can be heard running over the attic floor.
3. The boys can be seen playing in Mr. Glasgow's orchard.
4. Huge, smouldering bonfires can be observed in the distant field.
5. They were extremely tired, and the beginning of despair could be felt.
6. Off in the distance, apartment buildings can be seen clearly without binoculars.
7. The wine taster sniffed the aroma of the new wine.
8. The battling armies can be observed on the plains.
9. By the time I get to Kingston, my absence will be felt by her.
10. The exhaust from the buses is breathed by everyone in the closed terminal.

The re-write procedure for the expletive is similar to the one used for passive sense verbs. First, get rid of the *there is/there are* construction. Thus, the sentence

There are two Great Danes that guard the grounds at all times.

becomes the following word group:

two Great Danes that guard the grounds at all times

Make the fragment a sentence:

Two Great Danes guard the grounds at all times.

When an adjective clause or a participle phrase follows the subject, the new sentence can use the action of the subordination, as in the example above. However, sometimes the draft sentence won't give you the action, and you will have to supply your own verb. Here's an example:

> There are three cats in the yard.

Getting rid of the expletive leaves this word group:

> three cats in the yard

What do the cats do in the yard? Again, a dictionary of synonyms may be helpful. Here's a possible re-write:

> Three cats play in the yard.

Exercise 11.4 ∗

Re-writing Expletive Constructions

Instructions:

Each of the sentences below uses a *there is/there are* construction. Re-write each sentence to give the subject some action.

1. There is little time left.
2. There is a storm approaching from the west.
3. There were three men in the warehouse when it burned.
4. There is an old typewriter that needs repairs sitting up in the attic.
5. Mr. Jones' estate has good soil, but on Bill Smith's farm there are boulders and weeds and swamp.
6. There are seven turrets that surround the old castle.
7. There is a tremendous spirit on that team.
8. If the world food supply is not increased, there will be great despair.
9. There is only one man who can solve that problem.
10. There is a unique blend of the old and the new in their home.

The verb *to be* expresses a state of being. Its subjects do nothing; they just *are*. You should examine all your sentences that use only this verb. Try to find a better verb, one that gives the subject some action. For example, consider this sentence:

> The plant is by the window.

It doesn't show us what the plant is doing. The sentence might be re-written this way, instead:

The plant absorbs sunlight from the nearby window.

The re-write procedure is a familiar one. Get rid of the form of the verb *to be*. Then, ask yourself what the subject is doing. If the first verb you pull out of your head isn't the right one, take it to your dictionary of synonyms. Try each similar word in your sentence. Choose the one that says what you want to say.

However, don't fall into the trap. Sometimes the verb *to be* is the right word. Don't use replacement verbs that fuzzify your statement — verbs such as *seems, appears* or *looks*. Using these verbs to replace the verb *to be* suggests that you really don't know what you are writing about. For example, which sentence is the most direct?

John seems sick.
John is sick.

Certainly, the definite statement is more direct. Can you imagine Shakespeare considering this sentence?

To be or not to be, that seems to be the question.

His original sentence is more direct and definite:

To be or not to be, that is the question.

Exercise 11.5 *
Re-writing the Verb *To Be*

Instructions:

Re-write the sentences below. If it improves the sentence, replace the verb *to be* with a stronger, active verb.

1. The CN Tower is taller than any other structure in Toronto.
2. Between the house and the road are three mighty pine trees.
3. Research indicates that hitchhikers are a little more cautious now than a few years ago.
4. The bright red couch is in the dull living room.
5. The sentence in the example is from Shakespeare's *Hamlet*.
6. That magazine is as good a newsmagazine as any other.
7. The sportscaster is on at 6:40 p.m.
8. Your three cousins will be at the party.
9. Those books were all best sellers.
10. Florabelle is a wreck.

The Process Continues

The verbs in your sentences should express specific, definite action. When revising your draft sentences, look for these five weak constructions:

1. Long verb combinations
2. Passive verbs
3. Sense verbs in the passive voice
4. *There is/there are* constructions
5. Over-use of the verb *to be*.

Often a subordinate structure in the sentence will suggest an action verb. However, you will sometimes need to search for a word that makes your subject do something. Use a dictionary of synonyms to tap into your word bank.

Strong verbs have power and impact. Your entire composition will gain from this strength.

Review Assignment

Instructions:

Revise and re-write the weak verbs in the following paragraph. The focus and subordination have already been re-written; change them only if stronger verb power requires a change. Look for ten weak verb problems.

The living room of the celebrity's house is very impressive. A massive barn beam can be seen supporting and guarding the entrance on the southeast corner. In the southwest corner is a tall pine corner cupboard. The stone fireplace which dominates the south wall is 3 m across and solid to the ceiling. Across the room, in the northeast corner, there is a grand piano jutting into the room. There are four windows around the 8 by 10 m room. They start at waist level and climb to brass curtain rods suspended from the ceiling. Huge wall hangings in burlap and heavy orange and red wools are on the walls between the windows. Three Canadiana antiques —an old kitchen cupboard, a Québec bedroom chest which is used as a liquor cabinet, and a settle bed—line the walls. This arrangement does not make the room seem small. The middle of the room is filled by a 3 m long highback couch in white corduroy. Between the fireplace and the couch is a 3 m pine coffee table. Behind the couch can be seen an avocado tree climbing to the 4 m ceiling. This ceiling is stark white and untextured; this makes the room seem even larger. The heavy wool shag that covers the floor is in natural colours.

12

Completing Your Second Draft

Verb Correctness

Effective writing evolves. Effective writers manipulate the words in their draft sentences until all their sentences work. First, they review why each paragraph is there and what purpose it serves in the composition. This review directs the re-writing. Second, they examine the focus of each sentence and make sure that each sentence makes a strong statement. Third, they check and make their subordination correct and effective. Fourth, they re-write any weak verbs.

Checking for verb correctness is the fifth re-writing step. Not only must the verbs in your sentences be strong, but also they must be correct. The writer who labours over each sentence, who makes every word the right word, but who writes sentences such as the following, receives little credit:

> *Incorrect*   In November, the buds have went from the naked trees. On the ground, sodden leaves, laying in a brown heap, prepares for the first snow.

Instead, most readers cringe. Some may even dismiss the message, concentrating on the glaring errors. This chapter attacks incorrect verb use. Its purposes are the following:

1. To explain verb tenses and how to use them correctly.
2. To show how tenses are constructed and how to use a dictionary to find

the correct form for regular and irregular verbs.
3. To explain the problem of and solutions for incorrect subject/verb agreement.
4. To review the second draft process.

Verb Tenses

Verbs have different forms to indicate tense, and a verb's tense does two things. First, it tells your readers when events occur in time, whether they are in the past, the present or the future. Second, verb tenses show the time relationships among the events you are writing about, whether one event occurs before, during or after another event.

There are three common tense families—simple, progressive and perfect. The **simple** tenses are these:

I played   I play   I will play

Progressive tenses indicate that the entire action occurs over a period of time:

I was playing   I am playing   I will be playing

Perfect tenses express action that happened before something else:

I had played   I have played   I will have played

Different tenses are used to indicate present, past and future time. On the next page is a chart showing the use of each.

Your decision about which tense to use in any sentence depends on when the action of the sentence happens—in the present, in the past or in the future. If it's in the present, make sure the verb in the independent clause or emphasis shows present time. If it's in the past, the verb in the independent clause must show past time. The rule holds for future time as well.

If your sentence shows more than one event, use tenses to keep the time sequence clear. For example, the following sentence might be confusing:

John's putting improved; he bought a new putter.

Changing a tense expresses the relationship between the two statements more effectively:

John's putting improved; he had bought a new putter.

There are just a few rules associated with correct tense use. First, the present simple tense is used to express habitual action, action that steps over the boundaries of past, present and future:

> Jim Nelford *plays* golf.

Second, the present simple tense is used to express timeless facts:

> Water *boils* at 100°C.

VERB TENSES AND TIME	
Some verb tenses show present time:	
Simple present	I *play* golf.
Progressive present	I *am playing* golf.
Some verb tense show past time:	
Simple past	I *played* a good game yesterday.
Progressive past	I *was playing* when the storm struck.
Perfect present	I *have played* for many years.
Perfect past	I *had played* my game before he arrived.
Some verb tenses show future time:	
Simple present	I *play* in a tournament next month.
Simple future	I *will play* tomorrow.
Progressive present	I *am playing* a practice round next week.
Progressive future	I *will be playing* golf tomorrow when she comes.
Perfect future	I *will have played* before he arrives.

Exercise 12.1*

Verb Tenses

Instructions:

Each of the paragraphs below has verb tense problems. Re-write the verbs to clear up any confusion.

PARAGRAPH 1

Diary Entry

I am in Montréal, stayed at Place Bonaventure. My room faced the Place Ville-Marie. Below me in the evening lights, I saw the people moving across the patios. Some were in a hurry, others walk leisurely. I couldn't distinguish anything else as my room is on the seventeenth floor and it was even difficult to make out the sex of the pedestrians. The sun set quickly this evening. I watch it during my vigil. I watched it moving down to the tall buildings and the mountains that were in the west. Then it disappeared, as if some monster will eat it with a greedy gulp.

PARAGRAPH 2

Our new house will be ready in three months. Right now, the foundations were complete. It didn't look like the house of our dreams as it sits in the mud and rubble that construction sites will create. But we are enthusiastic. We could see the skeleton of our dream house. Yesterday we walked over the site with the architect's drawings. We use our imaginations. We see the living room furnished and hear the children playing in the family room downstairs. We have a magnificent house.

Regular and Irregular Verbs

An understanding of tense alone doesn't guarantee that your verbs will have the correct form. For example, the past tense of *play* is *played*. Shouldn't then the past tense of *go* be *goed*, and of *teach* be *teached*? Of course, that idea seems reasonable, but as you know, those forms are incorrect; the past tense of *go* is *went*, and of *teach* is *taught*.

Verb forms cause problems for many writers. But, they needn't. Here are the basics. First of all, every verb has four forms:

1. Base form
2. Past tense form
3. Past participle form
4. Present participle form.

The base form, the form listed in the dictionary, is used in the

present simple tense and, with the auxilliary *will*, in the **simple future** tense:

> The Smiths *play* bridge very well. Next week, they *will play* in the Edmonton tournament.

The past tense form is used in the **simple past** tense. That is the only time it is used:

> They *played* in Moncton last month.

The past participle form is combined with the simple tenses of the verb *have* in the three perfect tenses—the **perfect present**, the **perfect past** and the **perfect future**:

> They *have played* together for three years. Before that, they *had played* against each other in local clubs. By the end of the summer, they *will have played* in all the big Canadian tournaments.

The present participle form is used in the progressive tenses. The simple tenses of the verb *to be* are the linking verbs:

> They *are playing* in Windsor this week. They *were playing* the last rubber when I talked to them. They *will be playing* in the championship match when you arrive.

Every verb has these four forms, and these four forms are always used in these ways. Some verbs which are called **regular** add *ed* or *d* to the base form to make both the past tense form and the past participle form. Adding *ing* to the base form makes the present participle form. The verb *play* is a regular verb.

Countless other verbs are **irregular**; their four forms don't follow this regular pattern. One such verb is *see*. Its four forms are the following:

1. Base form: see
2. Past tense form: saw
3. Past participle form: seen
4. Present participle form: seeing

Once you know the four forms, writing the correct tense is easy. The simple tenses are these:

> I see   I saw   I will see

The progressive tenses are these:

> I am seeing   I was seeing   I will be seeing

And, the perfect tenses are these:

> I have seen   I had seen   I will have seen

Unfortunately, there's no key to identifying which verbs are regular and which are irregular. That knowledge comes with experience. There is, however, a tool used to find the correct form of any verb in question. A good dictionary lists any irregular forms of a verb.They are listed in this order: base form, past tense form, past participle form and present participle form. Here are a couple of entries from *The Gage Canadian Dictionary* that show how the irregular forms are listed:

> **ride** (rid) *v.* **rode** or *(Archaic)* **rid, rid-den** or *(Archaic)* **rid, rid-ing**, *n. — v.* **1** sit on a horse or other animal and make it go. **2** sit on a bicycle, etc. and make it go. **3** be carried along as if on horseback; be carried along by anything: *ride on a train*. **4** admit of being ridden: *a horse that rides easily*. **5** ride over, along, or through. **6** be mounted on; be carried on: *The eagle rides the winds*. **7** do or perform: *ride a race*. **8** move on; float; float along: *The ship rode the waves*. **9** *Informal*. make fun

> **drive** (driv) *v.* **drove** or *(Archaic)* **drave**, **driv-en, driv-ing**, *n. — v.* **1** make go: *Drive the dog away*. *Drive the nails into the board*. *Grief drove her insane*. **2** force (into or out of some place, condition, act, etc.): *Hunger drove him to steal*. **3** direct the movement of (an automobile, a horse-drawn vehicle, etc.). **4** go or carry in an automobile, carriage, etc. **5** carry out with vigor; bring about: *drive a bargain*. **6** work hard or compel to work hard. **7** dash or rush with force: *The ship drove on the rocks*. **8** set in motion; supply power for: *The wind drives the windmill*.

Check your own dictionary to see how it lists the forms of irregular verbs.

*Exercise 12.2 ***

Verb Forms

Instructions:

Some of the verb forms in the following sentences are incorrect. Fix them without changing the verb tense; change only the principle verb, not the auxiliary if one is included.

1. The new speedboat has ran into a snag.
2. The frozen water pipe had blew apart the night before.
3. I had laid down for a rest just before she arrived.
4. I had rode around before I met him.
5. I'm sure I lay the book on that shelf.

6. He told me that I'd better set down before he gives me the news.
7. She had mistook the girl for an old friend.
8. I have swam over a mile.
9. The temperature has rose over the last hour.
10. The trapper hanged the wolf carcass from a tree.

Subject/Verb Agreement

A verb must agree in number with its subject. Thus, the following sentence is incorrect; its plural subject doesn't agree in number with its verb:

> *Incorrect*   Dog teams travels the pipeline route.

Subject/verb agreement problems occur in the present simple tense, in the progressive tenses and in the present perfect tenses. And, many don't sound wrong. Here's another example of a subject/verb agreement error that occurs too frequently:

> *Incorrect*   Each of the natives search for ecological damage.

A writer who makes subject/verb agreement errors jeopardizes previous decisions. The focus of the sentence becomes unclear. The emphasis is incorrect, and subordinate structures are often made too important. These are all good reasons to check subject/verb agreement.

There are three subject/verb agreement rules:

1. A singular subject takes a singular verb form, and a plural subject takes a plural verb form.
2. Two or more subjects joined by the word *and* take the plural verb form.
3. Two or more subjects joined by *or* or correlative conjunctions take the verb form that agrees with the subject placed closest to the verb.

The first rule causes the most problems. First of all, you have to be certain you know what the singular and plural verb forms are. Verbs are different from nouns. If I want to form the plural of a noun, generally I simply add the letter *s*. Hence, one *team* becomes two *teams*. However, it doesn't work the same way with verbs. In the simple present tense, for instance, the singular verb form has an *s*. The plural form does not:

> The women's team *travels* by bus. On the other hand, the two men's teams *travel* by plane.

If you are ever unsure about what form to use, try this simple trick. If the subject is singular, substitute the word *it*, and then say the verb:

it
The team with the white huskies is driven by my friend.

And, if the subject is plural, substitute the word *they*:

they
Those people with the snowmobiles try to beat him all the time.

The next problem is recognizing which subjects are singular. The following words are always singular:

each, every, everyone, everybody, either, neither, anybody, anyone, nobody, no one

Any time one of these words acts as a subject, its verb must be singular:

Each of the natives searches for ecological damage.

Collective nouns are singular. Words such as *flock, faculty* and *team* take the singular verb form when the subject is acting as one:

The faculty is voting on the new contract.

Some nouns are complements; even when there are two, they are judged to be a singular subject:

Ham and eggs is the breakfast special.

The second rule recognizes that when you join two subjects with the word *and*, the subject is plural; it takes the plural verb form:

Kate and her friends are going to the movies.

But *and* is the only word that can act as an addition sign. Note the following example:

Paul, along with his friends, is meeting them after the show.

The third rule states that when you join two or more subjects with the word *or*, you must use the verb form that agrees with the subject closest to the verb. Here are some examples:

Bert or his parents are driving the van.

His parents or Bert is driving the van.

This same rule applies when you join two subjects with correlatives:

Neither he nor they drive very well.

Not only the students but also the faculty wants a settlement.

Most subject/verb agreement mistakes occur with two constructions. The first is when an adjective phrase comes between the subject and its verb:

Incorrect   Neither of the final exams were difficult.

The writer of this sentence has mistakenly made the verb agree with the word *exams*. Yet, the subject of the sentence is the word *neither*, a singular subject. The sentence should read this way:

Neither of the final exams was difficult.

The second construction to watch closely is when the verb is in an adjective clause. Here's an example:

Incorrect   He is one of those men who loves the north.

In this sentence, the adjective clause *who loves the north* is modifying *men*, not *one*. Therefore, the subject of the verb *love* is plural. The sentence should be this:

He is one of those men who love the north.

Exercise 12.3 *

Subject/Verb Agreement

Instructions:

Choose the correct verb form in the following sentences.

1. My interest in sports (goes, go) back to my childhood.
2. November or February (is, are) the best time to go south.
3. They (have, has) drunk too much.
4. There (was, were) a few sale items left.
5. The size and price of the book (has, have) been increased.
6. The builders or the architect (plans, plan) to see you in the morning.
7. Where (is, are) the nails and the hammer?
8. Mary, as well as her sister, (attends, attend) this school.
9. The seven books and the notebook (belongs, belong) to my sister.
10. Each of the men (is, are) talented.

11. (Are, is) there one or two *N*'s in her name?
12. She is one of those people who (believes, believe) in nuclear disarmament.
13. The realization of fame and fortune (causes, cause) problems for some people.
14. The desk with its ornate brassware and unusual accessories (is, are) for sale.
15. A flock of geese (is, are) flying over my house.

The Process Continues

The second draft process involves examining and if necessary re-writing every sentence. Your goal is to make strong statements that support or develop the point of the paragraph. By taking each paragraph in turn and going through the process—leaving what works and changing what doesn't—you improve your draft.

As a review of the second draft process, here's a step-by-step examination of how one writer revises and re-writes a draft paragraph.

First, she re-reads the paragraph, noting in the margin the purpose of the paragraph:

> One highlight of the fashion program at Sheridan is the number of fashion shows during the year that feature the creations of the program's students. Sometimes they are in other places, but generally you can see these exhibitions in Sheridan Hall. Sheridan Hall is the only large auditorium in the Oakville Campus. For a show, a large T-stage is set up on the floor of the auditorium. In front of the T, the models can see the judges that sit at the tables with bemused, startled or impressed looks that mark the students' creations. Behind the shaft of the T-stage, each girl, wearing new and interesting clothes, start her presentation. A backdrop protects the girls from the eyes of the audience who sometimes crowds the main floor. More often, the jocks and the business boys stand or sit in the upper level. It is most common to see bad art on the backdrop and the odd wilting plant drooping around the stage.

Setting of fashion shows

Second, she re-writes any weak focuses. Each focus should develop the point of the paragraph:

> One highlight of the fashion program at Sheridan is the number of fashion shows during the year that feature the creations of the program's students. Sometimes they are in other places, but generally ~~you can see~~ these exhibitions, *are* in Sheridan Hall. Sheridan Hall is the only large auditorium in the Oakville Campus. For a show, a large T-stage is set up on the floor of the auditorium. In front of the T, ~~the models can see~~ the judges ~~that~~ sit at the tables with bemused, startled or impressed looks that mark the students' creations. ~~Behind~~ *is the entrance where* the shaft of the T-stage, each girl, wearing new and interesting clothes, start her presentation. A backdrop protects the girls from the eyes of the audience who sometimes crowds the main floor. More often, the jocks and the business boys stand or sit in the upper level. ~~It is most common to see~~ bad art, *is* on the backdrop and the odd wilting plant droop*s*~~ing~~ around the stage.

Third, she examines all emphases and subordinate structures. She wants to make strong statements about her focuses, and she works to make her subordination effective and correct:

> One highlight of the fashion program at Sheridan is the number of fashion shows during the year, *These shows* ~~that~~ feature the creations of the program's students. ~~Sometimes~~ *although* they are *Sometimes* in other places, ~~but~~ generally these exhibitions are in Sheridan Hall, ~~Sheridan Hall is~~ the only large auditorium in the

Oakville Campus. For a show, a large T-stage is set up on the ~~floor of the auditorium~~. In front of the T, the judges~~sit~~ at the tables~~with~~~~bemused, startled or impressed ~~looks that mark the students' creations~~. The shaft of the T-stage is the entrance where each girl, wearing new and interesting clothes, start her presentation. A backdrop protects the girls from ~~the eyes of~~ the audience who ~~sometimes~~ crowds the main floor~~More often the jocks and the business boys stand or sit in~~ the upper level. Bad art is on the backdrop and the odd wilting plant droops around the stage.

Handwritten annotations above the paragraph: auditorium / who mark the students / These judges usually look / and

Finally, she examines each verb, first for strength and impact and then for correctness of tense, form and agreement:

~~One~~ highlight ~~of~~ the fashion program at Sheridan~~is~~ the number of fashion shows during the year. These shows feature the creations of the program's students. Although they are sometimes in other places, generally these exhibitions are in Sheridan Hall, the only large auditorium in the Oakville Campus. For a show, a large T-stage is set up on the auditorium floor. In front of the T, the judges who mark the students sit at the tables. These judges usually look bemused, startled or impressed. The shaft of the T-stage ~~is~~ the entrance where each girl, wearing new and interesting clothes, start her presentation. A backdrop protects the girls from the audience who crowd the main floor and the upper level. Bad art ~~is on~~ the backdrop and the odd wilting plant droops around the stage.

Handwritten annotations: serves as / s / adorns

Normally, you wouldn't need to write out each task as a separate draft. Instead, you've left plenty of room on your first draft for all your re-writing. Your second draft probably looks more like this:

> ~~One~~ highlight ~~of~~ the fashion program at Sheridan, is the
> number of fashion shows during the year ~~that~~ *These shows* feature the
> creations of the program's students. ~~Sometimes,~~ *although* they are, *sometimes* in
> other places, ~~but~~ generally ~~you can see~~ these exhibitions, *are* in
> Sheridan Hall, ~~Sheridan Hall is~~ the only large auditorium in
> the Oakville Campus. For a show, a large T-stage is set up on
> the *auditorium* floor ~~of the auditorium.~~ In front of the T, ~~the models can~~
> ~~see~~ the judges, ~~that~~ *who mark the students* sit at the tables, ~~with~~ *These judges usually look* bemused, startled or
> impressed ~~looks that mark the students' creations.~~ ~~Behind~~
> the shaft of the T-stage, *serves as the entrance where* each girl, wearing new and interesting
> clothes, starts her presentation. A backdrop protects the girls
> from ~~the eyes of~~ the audience who ~~sometimes~~ crowd the
> main floor. ~~More often the jocks and the business boys stand~~
> ~~or/sit in~~ *and* the upper level. ~~It is most common to see~~ bad art ~~on~~
> *adorns* the backdrop and the odd wilting plant drooping *s* around the
> stage.

Setting of fashion shows

Whatever it looks like, a successful second draft has strong sentences within well developed paragraphs. Here's our writer's final second draft in readable form. Note how it develops her point more effectively:

> The number of fashion shows during the year highlights
> the fashion program at Sheridan. These shows feature the
> creations of the program's students. Although they are
> sometimes in other places, generally these exhibitions are
> in Sheridan Hall, the only large auditorium in the Oakville

Campus. For a show, a large T-stage is set up on the auditorium floor. In front of the T, the judges who mark the students sit at tables. These judges usually look bemused, startled or impressed. The shaft of the T-stage serves as the entrance where each girl, wearing new and interesting clothes, starts her presentation. A backdrop protects the girls from the audience who crowd the main floor and the upper level. Bad art adorns the backdrop and the odd wilting plant droops around the stage.

Final Assignment

Instructions:

Use one of your pieces of writing and re-write it. Go through the second draft process.

13

Making Your Writing Flow

The Flow of Your Writing

Effective writing flows smoothly from sentence to sentence, from paragraph to paragraph. Effective writers work on their second drafts to make them unified compositions.

Unfortunately, second drafts don't always flow smoothly. Here's one writer's second draft paragraph:

> The course will help you in three ways. Your ability to read will improve. The course covers speed reading techniques. Your writing skills will be assessed. Your teacher will show you how to write more effectively. The course will examine your interpersonal skills—how well you deal with people.

The sentences are effective, but the paragraph is disjointed. While the subject matter is unified, the sentences are separated. In fact, the tone of the writing has suffered through the writer's second draft process.

This effect of re-writing sentences is common. Now is the time, however, to shape those sentences into a unified piece of prose. This chapter examines how to bring back the flow to your writing. Its purposes are the following:

1. To stress the importance of the sound of your writing.
2. To make you aware of the mistakes, especially in the use of pronouns, that block the flow of your writing.
3. To show you style devices that will improve the flow of your writing.

The Sound of Your Writing

Effective writers write as they speak. Listen to a best-selling author on a television or radio talk show. Although his or her speech is likely to be less precise, the sentences sound the same as when you read that author. That writer has worked hard to develop a personal style, one that is authentic and honest.

Undoubtedly, part of that work has been listening to the sound of sentences and noting how parts of the writing connect. You too will benefit from this part of every effective writer's process. **Read your writing out loud.** Don't whisper; let yourself hear how you've expressed yourself.

Of course, few of your readers will read your writing in this manner, but we are all more comfortable with writing that sounds right. We read it more easily. Why? Perhaps we remember how we learned to read—out loud. Also, we listen far more than we read or write, or even speak. We listen to the radio, to the television, to our teachers, to our co-workers. In fact, listening takes up more than half our waking hours. This familiarity with sound must affect how we read. We yearn for writing that sounds good and familiar.

The only way you can test for this rightness is to give your writing sound. While you listen to your writing, you can assess its tone and style. After assessment, you can improve the sound, or the flow, of your writing.

The writer whose paragraph you read at the beginning of the chapter read his writing out loud. Parts of it he didn't like. Here's his paragraph with some changes. Read it out loud, noting the improvements:

> The course will help you in three ways. First, your ability to read will improve since the course covers speed reading techniques. Also, your writing skills will be assessed and your teacher will show you how to write more effectively. Finally, the course will examine your interpersonal skills—how well you deal with people.

Fixing Transition Mistakes

In composition jargon, **transition** refers to the flow of writing. Writing with good transition moves forward; each sentence flows from the one before to the one after. On the other hand, ineffective transition impedes or blocks the flow of expression. The reader stops reading to figure out how one sentence fits with another, or why a sentence sounds wrong, or what a word refers to. Ineffective transition is the result of either mistakes or style problems. This section of the chapter examines the mistakes and how to fix them; the next section introduces style solutions.

The first two mistakes are easy to spot if you take the time to read your writing carefully. Sometimes, even the most experienced writer either **leaves out a word** or **repeats a word**. In a draft, mistakes like these are common:

Incorrect He sold horse at auction.
Incorrect The man who bought the horse lives in
in Calgary.

Using Pronouns Correctly

The third mistake, using pronouns incorrectly, requires more explanation. First, pronouns take the place of nouns; they function the same way. In fact, using pronouns is an excellent way to improve the flow of writing. Without pronouns, writers would have to repeat nouns constantly. Writing like this would result:

> Susie and Monica promised Joe and Ernie that Susie and Monica would come to Joe and Ernie's hideaway at midnight. When this writer asked the boys what the boys thought the chances were that the girls would come, Joe and Ernie replied that Joe and Ernie were sure the girls would arrive. "Susie and Monica are more daring than even Joe and Ernie," Joe said.

Each time you use a pronoun, it must point specifically to its antecedent, the noun that it replaces. If the pronoun does not agree and is not easily identified with its antecedent, you've made a mistake. Such incorrect pronoun use confuses your readers. If the antecedent is vague, remote or missing, readers stop reading and try to figure out what the sentence says. The flow of your writing stops.

A pronoun must agree with its noun antecedent in four ways:

Person: first, second or third
Number: singular or plural
Gender: masculine, feminine, or neuter
Case: subjective, objective, or possessive

A chart with the forms of the personal pronouns is given on page 138.

Most pronoun problems occur with case and number. They shouldn't if you keep some basics in mind. First, the pronoun takes the case for the place it assumes in the sentence. If the pronoun is the subject of a verb, then it takes the subjective form:

Susan and Julie flew to Winnipeg. *They* took an Air Canada flight.

If the pronoun shows possession, the possessive form is correct:

Their Uncle Jim met *their* flight.

All other positions in a sentence take the objective form of the pronoun:

He took *them* to their hotel.

Number problems, along with person problems, disappear if you keep your antecedents in mind. Here's the first of two common mistakes:

Incorrect   Each of the boys said they would help.

Re-write:

Each of the boys said he would help.

Here's the second common mistake:

Incorrect   My wife and I learned so many things, you couldn't remember them all.

Re-write:

My wife and I learned so many things we couldn't remember them all.

Currently, pronoun gender is the subject of much discussion. The old rule stated that, unless obviously inappropriate, the masculine form of the pronoun is used. Thus, a sentence such as this example was correct:

Each doctor issued his bills through the provincial medical plan.

Today, that sentence is inappropriate. Try to avoid such sentences. The following sentence says the same thing:

The doctors issued their bills through the provincial medical plan.

Avoid writing sentences with vague, remote or missing antecedents. When the antecedent is unclear, the sentence is confusing:

Incorrect   He told his brother that his car was wrecked.

Whose car was wrecked? Was it the car of *he* or the *brother*? Such a sentence should be re-written in this way:

He told his brother Sam that Sam's car was wrecked.

Another mistake to watch for is using a pronoun that refers to an

Forms of Personal Pronouns

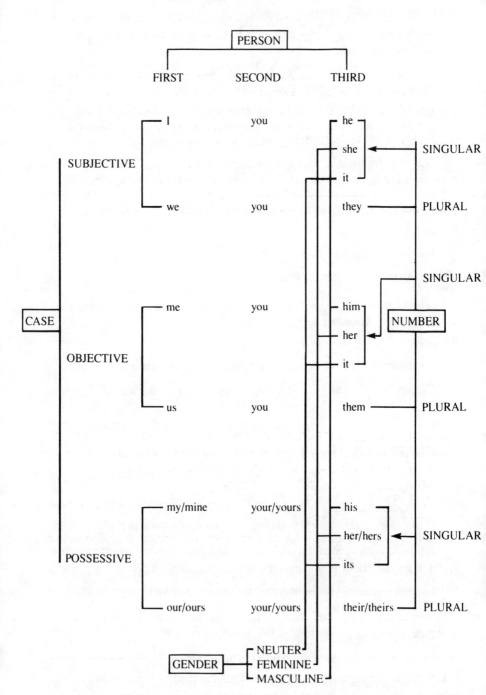

antecedent several sentences back. Here's an example:

> The accident occurred two days before. Sam had lent John the car to take his date home. While he was rounding a curve, the car's tire blew. John was lucky to escape from *it*.

The pronoun *it* refers to the word *accident* back in the first sentence. A reader would have to stop reading to sort this confusion out. Try to keep all antecedents no further than a sentence away from their pronouns.

Finally, make sure that your pronouns do refer to an antecedent. Don't write sentences like the second one in this example:

> *Incorrect*   Sam wants to be a mechanic. He gets a lot of practice at *it*.

It has no antecedent, so the sentence is vague in meaning. Make sure that your pronouns have antecedents and help the flow of your writing.

Exercise 13.1*

Pronouns

Instructions:

The following sentences have pronoun mistakes. Fix the pronoun problems.

1. Jan and Lori met to discuss the failure of her business.
2. Bill's father is a scientist, but Bill is not interested in it.
3. Fourteen cars piled up on the Trans-Canada Highway, but it did not hurt anyone.
4. Everyone at the party enjoyed themselves.
5. The teacher accused we students of being impolite.
6. Everyone except Roger and I was on time for the game.
7. Sheila is as tall as me.
8. Students writing tests often become very nervous. Therefore, I think they should be abolished.
9. The trapper charged a lot of money for the ermine's skin because they are hard to catch.
10. Each of the plumbers cast his ballot for the new contract.

Transition Devices

While these three transition mistakes block the flow of your writing, other problems in a second draft often restrict the transition of sentences. These style problems are rarely mistakes; instead, they offend the ear, or they get in the way of the logical progression of your writing. The three most common problems are the following:

1. Repeating the same word
2. Sentence sameness
3. Lack of a logical connection between sentences and paragraphs.

Word Repetition Problems

Often, substituting a pronoun for a noun overcomes word repetition problems:

> The *dog* barked because the *dog* wanted out.

Re-write:

> The dog barked because it wanted out.

Sometimes, however, the pronoun is inappropriate. Instead, you need to search for a synonym, a word that means the same thing. Here's an example:

> Captain Courage led his men into the *battle*. When the *battle* was over, he carried them out.

Re-write:

> Captain Courage led his men into the battle. When the *action* was over, he carried them out.

When you hear the same word repeated and you don't like the sound, write in a substitute. Again, use a dictionary of synonyms to spark your memory.

But, don't re-write every repeated word. Sometimes, repetition forges a link between sentences:

> Acme Industries will install a new *computer* to maintain quality control, to store accounts information and to make profit/loss reports. The *computer* will be operational in six weeks.

And sometimes, repetition is used for a good effect:

> He was almost finished, but he wanted to nail down in the clearest possible language his vision of the railway and his vision of the nation. He wanted, he said, an arrangement "which will satisfy all the loyal, legitimate aspirations, which will give us a great and united, a rich and improving, developing Canada, instead of making us tributary to American bondage, to American tolls, to American freights, to all the

little tricks and big tricks that American railways are addicted to for the purpose of destroying our road.''

(from *The National Dream* by Pierre Berton, used by permission of The Canadian Publishers, McClelland and Stewart Limited, Toronto)

Sentence Sameness Problems

These problems take two forms. Either the sentences are all more or less the same length, or they are all constructed the same way. Both problems lead to a monotony of sound. The writing takes on a singsong rhythm, or perhaps a constant bump, bump—like the wheels of a train over an uneven track. If you hear these patterns, here's what to do.

If your sentences are all long, break one up into two smaller sentences. But, don't break them all up—if you do, you will have a succession of short sentences, an equally annoying problem:

> The dam was built in 1973. It was designed to produce hydroelectricity. The lake that was created is now a recreational area. People from the area enjoy swimming and boating.

With a series of short sentences, subordinate the least important emphasis. Here's a possible re-write:

> The dam was built in 1973. It was designed to produce hydroelectricity. The lake that was created is now a recreational area where people enjoy swimming and boating.

Repetitive sentence structure problems come in many forms, but the most common is the *emphasis/subordination* pattern. The problem is compounded when the subordination takes the same form. Here's an example:

> A pot-bellied stove sits in the west corner of the kitchen. An old cane chair rests against the opposite wall. The old black dog lies at the doorway.

Each sentence has an emphasis followed by an adverb phrase. One way to improve the sound of the passage is to move the subordination. Adverbial subordination can go before the main clause. Here's a possible re-write:

> A pot-bellied stove sits in the west corner of the kitchen. Against the opposite wall rests an old cane chair. The old black dog lies at the doorway.

This re-write places two references to space closer together. Look for time relationships that can be grouped in a similar way:

> You turn the clocks forward in the spring. You turn them back in the fall.

Re-write:

> You turn the clocks forward in the spring. In the fall, you turn them back.

Another style device that improves sentences is using variety in your subordinate structures. Note what adjective forms you are using. For instance, I use adjective clauses too often. Here's an example:

> The car *that was belching smoke and making whirring noises* pulled into the garage.

When I re-write, I search for them and sometimes make them participle phrases:

> *Belching smoke and making whirring noises*, the car pulled into the garage.

Or, I turn the subordinate clause into a main clause:

> *The car belched smoke and made whirring noises* when it pulled into the garage.

Of course, some adjective clauses that I like I leave.

Exercise 13.2

Sentence Sameness

Instructions:

In each of the following questions, there is a sentence sameness problem. Re-write the passages to make the sentences flow.

1. Gerry went to college in Toronto because he wanted to stay at home while his brother played his final year of hockey with the Marlboros. The previous year, Gerry had been one of the regular patrons of the Marlboro home games and he didn't want to leave the city when the team was about to have a good year.
2. Last night, I went to a hamburger stand for dinner. The night before, I ate take-out chicken.
3. In 1976, Bobby Orr finally played international hockey. He scored two goals in the Canada Cup. He had seven assists. He played with style and controlled the play. He was named the outstanding player in the tournament.

4. I am sitting at a desk in the middle of the library. Another student is working directly in front of me.
5. The rectangle is divided in two halves, horizontally. A triangle is inside the rectangle. The triangle rises from the bottom corners of the rectangle. The top angle of the triangle is in the middle of the top line of the rectangle.
6. One new teaching resource is the audio-tutorial program. The student listens to information on tape. Exercises that test new skills are provided in a workbook. Important information is repeated in print. The instructor can spend time working with individual problems.

Lack of Logical Connections

Although a primary purpose of your pre-writing is to logically connect information, sometimes draft sentences don't sound as if they belong together. Or, a paragraph doesn't fit with the paragraph that comes before. Often, you can group space or time relationships to force the connection. For example:

> At the beginning of the golf season, my game is terrible. By the fall, it has improved.

Re-write:

> My golf game is terrible at the beginning of the season. By the fall, it has improved.

Transitional words and phrases, by themselves or with subordination, are another transition device. Such words and phrases make the connection between sentences. Consider these two sentences:

> John went to hockey school in Prince Edward Island. His brother Harry went there.

They are brought together with the word *also*:

> John went to hockey school in Prince Edward Island. His brother Harry went there *also*.

Transitional words and phrases are also used to show differences, or contrast:

> *However*, their sister Hilary taught speed skating at a camp in Haliburton, Ontario.

And, they are used to make the connection when sentences indicate emphasis, example, consequence or restatement. These are some of the most common transitional words and phrases:

1. Similarity or Likeness

similarly, and, again, likewise, also, second, third, furthermore, finally, in addition, moreover

2. Difference or Contrast

but, however, to the contrary, on the other hand, nevertheless, although, conversely, still

3. Emphasis

chiefly, equally, indeed, even more important

4. Example

for example, as an example, for instance, specifically, that is, such as

5. Consequence

thus, then, so, it follows, as a result, hence, therefore

6. Restatement

in short, in effect, that is, in other words

When a paragraph doesn't connect with the end of the previous paragraph, you have two options. You could use sentence transition devices to connect the two sentences—the last of the first paragraph and the first of the second paragraph—or, write a transition sentence to connect the two paragraphs. Here's an example that uses a transition sentence:

> We may eventually see the day where a golfer will carry three different colours in his bag and then decide which one he wants to use depending on the weather, season or condition of the course. For example if the rough was particularly long on a given day, the player may choose to use one of the high visibility balls to cut down on the amount of time that he spends searching for stray shots.
>
> **Optometrists will be the first to tell you that golf balls painted yellow or orange are unquestionably easier to see than their white counterparts.**
>
> "White is not a colour, but rather an absence of colour," according to Dr. Brian Feldman who is chairman of the Sports Vision Committee of the Ontario Association of Optometrists. "The eye is a contrast detector. Yellow is the most visible colour because of contrast sensitivity. It is the colour that is naturally seen brightest by the human eye, and against a dark turf background yellow would appear as the most visible.

Both yellow and orange are considerably brighter than white because white offers little or no contrast.''

(from ''Optic Balls: Fad or Fixture?'' by Rob Longley, published in *Score*, Canada's Golf Magazine, June/July, 1982)

Exercise 13.3

Transitional Words

Instructions:

In each of the following questions, the sentences have transition problems. Use transitional words or phrases to solve the problems.

1. To write effectively, several skills are important. You must learn how words work. You must anticipate your readers. You must organize logically. You must present your writing in well-crafted sentences that flow.
2. The new car can be manufactured for less than $4500. The engine is made of aluminum and the body is fiberglass. Gasoline ratings state that it travels 100 km on 5.2 L of gas.
3. Many writing problems are individual. Some people cannot identify spelling problems; others are baffled by punctuation.
4. He studied for three hours every night of the semester. He didn't miss more than five classes in all his courses. He received no less than a B+ on every assignment. I propose he win the Dean's Medal.
5. Their new house has four bedrooms, three baths and a family room on the second floor. The ground floor boasts a living room, kitchen, dining room, two bathrooms and a complete master bedroom suite. A billiards room and a small movie theatre, complete with a bar and lined with sofas, is downstairs. The house is impressive.

The Process Continues

Read your second draft out loud. Watch and listen for these problems:

1. Words that are left out.
2. Words that are repeated.
3. Pronouns that are used incorrectly.
4. The same word being used too often.
5. Sentences that are the same length or have the same structure.
6. The lack of logical connections between sentences or paragraphs.

The first three problems are mistakes; they must be corrected. The last three problems generally block the flow of your writing; they should be corrected, too.

When you work on the transition of your draft sentences, keep three cautionary notes in mind:

1. Sometimes, fixing transition problems can cause other, possibly worse, problems.
2. Sometimes, you don't want transition.
3. Rely on your own ear. It's your style you are improving.

Final Assignment

Instructions:

Use the second draft you prepared for Final Assignment, Chapter 12 and work on the flow of your writing.

14

Preparing Your Final Copy

Rules and Formats

Effective writing follows the rules. Effective writers recognize the advantages of these rules and guides: they are accepted by both reader and writer. Thus, a writer who uses a punctuation mark correctly knows that its use signals a particular construction. A specific word, spelled in the accepted way, has a meaning that the reader either knows or can discover in a dictionary. A grammar rule has evolved as the most efficient way to make a statement clearly and concisely.

No effective writer can escape the limitations of the accepted rules. You can't disregard the properties of a sentence, the use of commas, or the correct spelling of a word. But, don't think that these rules are constant. The rules that you and I follow are different from those that Chaucer, Shakespeare, Dickens or even Leacock followed. Dictionaries, grammar books, handbooks (and teachers) only document these changes; they don't make them. The rules change because the language and the world it represents change. Effective writers understand the rules first. Then, they reach beyond them when necessary.

This chapter looks at rules and formats, the last stage of the writing process. The purposes of this chapter are the following:

1. To outline a specific final grammar check.
2. To introduce a basic punctuation guide.

3. To stress the importance of correct spelling and to explain how to work towards improving your spelling.
4. To give some guidelines about the appearance of your final copy.

Check Your Grammar—Again

The last seven chapters have examined the basic rules of grammar as part of your writing process. You've seen how the grammatically correct way to write something is also the most effective way to express that idea. Your final draft sentences should go through a final grammar check. Here's a quick review of what you've studied:

GRAMMAR CHECK	
1. Make sure each sentence is a correct **sentence unit.**	Pages 70-74
Avoid sentence **fragments**	Pages 74-76
Avoid **run-on sentences**	Pages 77-78
2. Make sure your **subordination** has the right form and is positioned correctly.	Pages 96-99
Avoid **using an adjective to function as an adverb**	Page 100
Avoid **misplaced subordination**	Page 101
Avoid **dangling subordination**	Page 101
3. Use **parallelism** correctly.	Pages 104-106
4. Make sure your **verbs** are correct.	
Check the **verb tense**	Pages 121-122
Check the **verb form**	Pages 123-125
Check **subject/verb agreement**	Pages 126-128
5. Make sure your **pronouns** agree with their antecedents.	Pages 136-139

Exercise 14.1*

Grammar Review

Instructions:

Each of the sentences below has an error. Determine what kind of error has been made and fix each one.

Example:

Your inquiry about the order received yesterday.

Answer:

We received your inquiry about the order yesterday. (Problem — sentence fragment; Correction — as above)

1. Your order of belt buckles were shipped yesterday.
2. Your sales representative told us to send it to Kamloops, however, the order specified it should be sent to Red Deer.
3. Our representative visits your area last week.
4. He told Mr. Smith that his proposal had been turned down.
5. That proposal was an interesting one. He promised to give jobs to everyone, to lower the cost of living and increasing the profits of local businesses.
6. The seminar is held in the conference room which has an agenda posted on the bulletin board.
7. Although the schedule of events may change.
8. Each taxpayer receives the booklet they need to complete their returns.
9. Using the booklet, your tax return is easy to complete.
10. The accuracy of the returns has improved noticeable.

Correct and Effective Punctuation

In case you consider punctuation unimportant, try reading the following passage without it:

That that is is that that is not is not is that it it is

Only the correct punctuation gives it meaning:

That, that is, is. That, that is not, is not. Is that it? It is!

Punctuation marks point the way. Just as traffic signals make driving safer and more organized, punctuation marks indicate your sentence constructions and clarify your meaning. Correct punctuation tells your readers when to stop and when to go.

The following rules are basic to the use of commas, semicolons, quotation marks, apostrophes and end marks. They certainly are not the complete rules. Always use a writer's handbook to check whenever you aren't sure about the use of punctuation.

Commas are the most frequently used punctuation mark. They separate constructions within a sentence. For example, they **separate the independent clauses** in a sentence. Always put a comma before the coordinating conjunction in a sentence with two independent clauses:

> James likes reading, but his wife prefers watching movies.

Commas **separate introductory subordination** from the independent clause. Subordination before the independent clause can be either a clause or a phrase and is generally more than three words long:

> Often when he is reading, she will go and watch a movie on television.

However, subordination after the independent clause is not separated by a comma:

> He doesn't even notice her absence when she leaves the room.

Commas **separate parallel elements** in a sentence:

> His wife is a happy, funny and lovable person.
> On Saturdays, you will find her playing the guitar, singing popular songs and dancing with the kids at the youth center.
> She won a special citizen's award because she persuaded some of her friends to be volunteers, because she raised money for the center and because the kids all like her.

Commas are also used to **separate words or constructions that are not essential to the sentence's meaning**. These additions can be transitional words or phrases:

> James, however, is a bore.

They can also be complete clauses:

> Carol, who works for a mortician, says that he can be fun sometimes.

From your study of sentences, you know that a **semicolon** is used to join two or more independent clauses in one sentence; this use is the most frequent. Make sure you use semicolons correctly in your final copy:

> He once went to a rock concert; he enjoys a lot of popular music.

A **colon** is used to introduce a list. For example:

His wife once listed his qualities: generosity, kindness, tolerance, understanding and tidiness.

When you want to quote material from another person or another source, use **quotation marks** around that material. However, be sure that you use quotation marks only around a direct quotation, not around a paraphrase.

I've often heard Carol say, "I think he's a wonderful husband."

Watch your use of the **apostrophe**. It is used in two ways. First, to show possession, the apostrophe is added to the noun which does the possessing. (Don't forget a noun is a person, place or thing.) For example:

I saw him at his best friend's house.

In the above example, the friend owns the house. The apostrophe indicates that possession.

Many writers have problems dealing with plural possessives. Here's a trick. To show possession, always add on *s* to the noun which possesses — whether that noun is singular or plural. If you ever have an *s's*, just get rid of the last *s*. Here are two examples of correct apostrophe use:

He joined the men's gossiping.
He laughed at all the ladies' jokes.

Second, apostrophes are used in contractions. The apostrophe is inserted where letters have been taken from words. Hence:

He *can't* help it if he sometimes seems dull.

In this example, the apostrophe takes the place of the letters *no* in the word *cannot*.

Don't forget your end marks. A **period** ends a statement or command. A **question mark** ends a direct question, and an **exclamation mark** is used to end a sentence which expresses strong feeling or surprise.

Check Your Spelling

Nothing discredits a writer more than a misspelled word. Employers, teachers and peers cringe when confronted with incorrect spelling. I've seen colleagues ridiculed, books rejected and careers limited because of misspelled words. Regrettably, it sometimes seems as if writing and expression are just spelling and nothing more.

These are reasons enough to mind your spelling. But, even more important is this one: often a misspelled word causes real confusion. For example, in the following sentence the writer is talking about garments:

Your cloths will be ready in three weeks.

However, the incorrect spelling of the word *clothes* suggests that only the cloth for the garments will be ready in three weeks, not the clothes themselves.

The first skill to work on is the ability to recognize misspelled words. When you proofread, you are not reading for meaning, for the two kinds of reading are very different. When you read for meaning, you only see the shapes of words; when you proofread, you narrow your gaze to the actual letters and how they are put together. Here are two good tricks that force you to proofread each word:

1. Block off the word before and after the word you are reading.
2. Read backwards—from the last word to the first word.

Both methods of proofreading force you to look at how the words are constructed rather than at what the words are saying.

Of course, finding a spelling error in your draft sentences is only half the battle; now, you have to spell the word correctly. For some, this task is fairly easy—go to the dictionary and find the correct spelling of the word. But for others, the job is not so easy. They ask, "How can I find the word in the dictionary when I can't spell the word?" Students sometimes come to me exasperated. I remember one who knew he had spelled *psychology* incorrectly, yet his efforts to find the word under *s* had been terribly frustrating.

If you have trouble with spelling, here are some suggestions. Purchase a speller's dictionary, a resource book listing words by how they are commonly misspelled. In such a book, the word *psychology* is listed under *s* as well as under *p*. Also, a good writer's handbook lists commonly misspelled words and words that sound alike or look alike. A programmed spelling text may be useful. These texts offer a self-paced spelling program; many of them let you test yourself as you go along. They cover basic rules and, if you work with them, may make the task of proofreading a little easier.

The best solution, however, is to build your own spelling resource book. Most poor spellers have trouble with the same or the same kind of words. So, buy a small pocket-size notebook, label each page with a letter from A to Z, and keep track of the words you misspell. When you proofread, refer to your notebook. In time, you won't need it; you'll know how to spell your trouble words.

Finally, proofread like a pro. The inexperienced writer proofs something once and thinks that that's adequate. The professional writer proofs a piece over and over—perhaps as many as eight times. Any word that he or she suspects is misspelled is circled to be checked before the final draft is prepared. Remember, your job is to find any misspelled words so that your final copy will be error-free. It's far better to check twenty words to find only four that are wrong than to check only three and leave the fourth incorrect.

*Exercise 14.2 ***

Proofreading

Instructions:

Proof and correct the following draft paragraphs. Underline the words you change and circle the punctuation marks you add or delete.

> The first thing you should check when you by a puppy, is the temperment of the dog. One principal I have found sound is too check the sire or dame. If they are freindly, then the puppy will probably be alright. Another thing you should examine is the bone structure. Put the dog in a stationery poisition and feel him make sure the hips are not lose. This check is expecialy important because of the risk of hip dispacia.
>
> You should definitly consider you're facilitys. Don't forget that that cute little puppy will grow up and might not be so cute. This advise is good because some dogs have to have a great deal of exercise and some big dogs such as St. Bernerds or Great Danes cost a small fortune to feed. Finally, the forth point is that you should have the puppy checked by a veterinarian. This council could save you money and aggrava-sion. Of coarse, no vet can prophecy weather or not a little puppy will be a long-living, healthy dog, but he can check for puppy problems. Let the vet effect your decision. Don't throw away mony just becuase you feel sorry for a cute little puppy.

Your Final Copy

Make the copy you hand to your readers look good. A piece of writing that makes a good visual impression is always well received. Readers want to give it more attention, for the writer has obviously taken time and trouble to put it together.

What your final copy looks like depends on the writing problem. You should always check with your readers about the format of your final copy. Teachers generally have specific guidelines for essays and other assignments. Larger businesses and organizations have models for internal memos, external letters and different kinds of reports. Most publishing companies have manuscript guidelines that explain the form that writing pieces should take. If your readers don't specify a format model, check your library for letter, essay, report or manuscript models.

No matter what the format, effective writers follow some simple final copy guidelines. If you want your writing to look its most effective, it should be typed and double-spaced. If typing is either impossible or unnecessary, then write as neatly as you can. Use white-out to correct mistakes. Always double-space your writing and use only one side of the piece of paper.

Make sure you use the paper well. Don't make your writing look cramped; always use margins on all four sides of the paper. Check to make sure that each page is numbered at a consistent place on the page (probably the upper right-hand corner) and that pages are ordered correctly. Generally, some kind of binding holds the papers together. A simple fold, a staple or paper clip, or a cover that binds the left edges are all possibilities. Find out which method is appropriate.

The Process Ends

After you've made your writing flow, it's time to prepare your final copy.

1. Check the grammar of all sentences.
2. Check all punctuation.
3. Check the spelling.
4. Prepare your final copy following a model format.
5. Be proud of your work.

Final Assignment

Instructions:

Prepare the final copy of the piece you worked on for Final Assignment, Chapter 13.

15

Using Your Writing Process

Effective Writing

Effective writing works. And, an effective writing process helps you make your writing work; it leads the way as you attack any writing assignment. So, rather than staring at a blank piece of paper and waiting for inspiration, the effective writer knows how to proceed—what to do first and how to continue, from that first stage of defining the writing problem to the last stage of preparing the final copy.

Every writing problem calls for some modifications in the basic process. Some assignments require more time for gathering material; some, like exam questions, leave little time for extensive re-writing; and some become so straightforward that the writer can combine stages in the process. All of these refinements come with experience. The process becomes your writing process.

This chapter examines five different writing assignments. It concentrates on the writing problems and the necessary applications in the pre-writing stage of the process. The purposes of the chapter are the following:

1. To inform about writing exam questions.
2. To explain the pre-writing process for writing personal experience and opinion pieces and for research essays.
3. To show how to write letters of application and complaint.

Writing Exam Questions

Many exam writers read the question on the exam and start writing immediately. Sometimes, they think that their task is to write steadily and to write as many words as possible. However, this practice is ineffective, and the reasoning behind it is faulty.

Let's define the three variables of the writing problem. First, the what of the writing problem is given; either you've studied and you know the information, or you don't. Let's assume you've prepared yourself; you have the material and are ready to communicate it. Why do you write exam questions? Silly question, right? You have to, if you want to pass. Let's be even more positive. In terms of a successful result, you write exam questions to get top marks.

The who of the writing problem is the key. First, you know that your reader has the answers. Very probably, your writing will be graded against a marking scheme. Just as likely, this marking scheme lists the information you should include in your answer. Marking schemes are highly organized. They don't ramble; neither should your answer. Your reader is looking for a reasoned piece of writing that is controlled and organized. That's what earns top marks.

So, how do you write such a piece in the limited amount of time you have? You use your time productively. You do more thinking than writing.

Exam questions ask a question or make a statement that you are asked either to agree or disagree with, to comment upon or to explain. In all cases, you are given both the statement of purpose and the control statement. Don't stray away from these. The exam question is quite specific about what you are to write about. Your job is to develop the given control statement.

For example, here's an exam question from a first year economics test:

Explain how demand affects the price of a good or service.

The statement of purpose is this, therefore:

To inform my teacher about how demand affects the price of a good or service.

And, the control statement might be this:

When supply remains unchanged, increased demand raises the price of a good or service, and decreased demand lowers the price of a good or service.

The exam answer would develop these statements.

Once you've established the statement of purpose and your control statement, you can begin to pattern your answer. Use the pattern to structure and limit your information. Use half the time you have budgeted for the question to pre-write. Develop your answer adequately and organize your writing.

When your pattern is a pre-writing plan, write your exam answer. Don't puff it; just turn your plan into prose with the same straightforward tone you'd use if it were an oral exam. When you've finished your draft, and if you have time, read it over and correct any major problems. Generally, you won't have enough time to go through a complete re-writing process, but you should check for major grammatical errors that may confuse what you're saying. Check spelling as well.

Using Your Writing Process to Write Exam Questions

1. Use your time productively. Plan your time and try to allow half your time for pre-writing.
2. Write your statement of purpose and control statement from the exam question.
3. Use a pattern to structure the material you plan to use. Develop and organize your answer.
4. Write a draft. Don't shoot the bull; simply turn your plan into prose.
5. Check for grammar and spelling problems with the time you have left.

Writing Personal Experience Pieces

Personal experience pieces include opinions, reviews, progress reports and explanations of how to do something or of how something happened. They are the bulk of daily writing—the memos, the letters and the reports.

You write a personal experience piece because someone wants or needs to know about your experiences or your opinions. Generally, such pieces require little research although you may want to check facts and figures.

Using Your Writing Process to Write Personal Experience Pieces

1. Define the writing problem: What are you writing about? Who are you writing to—what do your readers know about your topic; how can you

help them to learn more? Why are you writing? Again, think of your readers—why do they want or need this information?

2. Brainstorm. This first effort may be similar to a first draft, especially if you are clear about the topic and what you want to say. When you are stating an opinion in your piece, use this time to get your thoughts down on paper.

3. You may want to build a working thesis after jotting down your ideas, especially if you need to check some information or get more material. However, you can probably write your statement of purpose and control statement immediately, and go directly to a pattern.

4. Build a pattern of your information. Develop your piece, thinking always of your purpose and your readers.

5. Plan your writing: create a pre-writing plan.

6. Write your first draft. If your readers are expecting your piece of writing, make sure your introduction clearly states your purpose. If your piece needs to attract readers, write an introduction that speaks to their needs—tell your readers how your piece will help them.

Writing Assignment 15.1

A How-To Piece

Instructions:

Write a how-to piece on a hobby or a particular skill that you have. Your readers should be able to do something after they've read your piece.

Writing Assignment 15.2

An Opinion Piece

Instructions:

Write an opinion piece about a movie you've seen recently. (Your finished piece should be about 500 words.)

Writing Research Papers

Writing a research paper is an opportunity to learn something. Most of your time is spent reading and collecting material to support a thesis. Effective research papers are full of information. They are well controlled and well organized. As well, they flow like a unified piece, not like a collection of other people's writings.

Writing a research paper is a scholastic exercise. Your effectiveness is based on four important tasks: 1) making a control statement about your topic—this is called your thesis; 2) collecting and organizing your material to support the idea expressed in your thesis; 3) weaving this information together into a piece of good writing; 4) scheduling your writing process. Often, the biggest difference between an effective and an ineffective research paper is how well the writer has managed time. Your writing process must help you limit your topic to a suitable thesis, collect material, and write a well-structured piece, all within the time period your instructor allows. Build yourself a deadline schedule and follow it.

Using Your Writing Process to Write a Research Paper

1. Define the writing problem: identify the who and understand the why. The what is the key to the assignment because you are often given a choice. Choose a topic that interests you, that you have some opinions about, and that you want to learn more about.
2. Brainstorm. Your objective is to build a working thesis and to limit your topic to a manageable assignment. It may be necessary to do some preliminary reading.
3. Research. This stage will take the most time. Here's how to go about it. First, go to your library's subject catalogue and make a list of all the books on your topic. Second, use the periodical indexes to find any magazine and periodical articles on your topic; add them to your list. Third, check out any other media resources, such as film strips, audio and video cassettes, your libraries have. When you add these to your list, you have prepared your preliminary bibliography.

   Next, collect all these sources—the books, the available articles, and the media resources. Your job now is to discover which ones will be useful; some won't be. With the books, read the introductions or prefaces, the tables of contents, and the indexes to find out if the books have information that will support your working thesis. Skim the articles to discover the same thing. Check over the media resources.

   Finally, take notes from the useful sources. Write down all the information you can. Keep track of where you find the material and on what pages of the source. Some writers use file cards (recipe size) for notetaking. On each card, you write the relevant information and the source.

4. When you've exhausted your sources, review what you've learned and write your statement of purpose and your control statement. Your control statement is your thesis.

5. Build a pattern of your information. If you have used cards, this stage of the process can be easier. Arrange the cards in appropriate groups and consider each card as a branch in your pattern. Then use your pattern to review your thesis and the adequacy of your research.

6. Plan your paper: create a pre-writing plan.

7. Write your first draft. Work to make your writing flow and to integrate any quotations you are using into your piece. Your introduction should interest your readers and state your thesis; your conclusion should summarize the main points you have used to support your ideas.

8. The final copy of your paper will have a formal title page, a bibliography page and footnotes. Footnotes give the source for all information that you have either quoted directly or paraphrased. Only information that is common knowledge in the field is not footnoted; therefore, most of your paper must be footnoted. Make sure that you use a consistent footnoting style. Many style guides are available, but your instructor might recommend one in particular. Your bibliography lists all the sources you have used to write your paper. Again, follow a standard bibliography format.

Writing Assignment 15.3

A Research Paper

Instructions:

Write a 1500 word research paper on one of the topics listed below. Create a deadline schedule that tells you when to complete each of the following stages of the process:

1. Working Thesis
2. Pre-writing Plan
3. First Draft
4. Final Copy

Here are the topics. Some have already been broken down—in such cases, choose only one part of the topic.

1. Abortion
2. The aged or aging
   a) housing
   b) problems of aging

    c) income
    d) sexuality

3. Alcohol and alcoholism
    a) effects of alcohol
    b) effect of an alcoholic parent on children
    c) addiction of women
    d) teenagers and alcohol

4. Astrology

5. Brain
    a) research
    b) brain damage

6. Consumerism
    a) education
    b) protection
    c) behaviour

7. Creativity

8. Cruelty to childen

9. Death
    a) psychological reactions
    b) cultural reactions

10. Demonology

11. Divorce

12. Drug abuse

13. Ecology

14. Family
    a) family life
    b) family institution
    c) marriage

15. Feminism

16. Juvenile delinquency

17. Nationalism

18. Nuclear technology
    a) nuclear power
    b) nuclear war
    c) nuclear weapons

19. Nutrition

20. Pollution

21. Sex
    a) customs
    b) crimes
    c) differences between the sexes
    d) sexual discrimination
    c) sexual roles

22. Technology and civilization

23. Violence on television and in film

24. Witchcraft

25. Women
    a) changing roles
    b) employment
    c) rights

26. Work
    a) nature of work
    b) work ethic

Writing Letters of Application

A letter of application often accompanies your résumé or data sheet. A well-written letter shows how your experiences and education can help a specific reader when that person tries to fill a job opening. A good letter of application can get you a job interview.

Before writing your letter, find out about the job and the company you are applying to. Finding this information might require some research. If you are responding to a specific advertisement or posting, on the other hand, the information will probably be printed.

Using Your Writing Process to Write a Letter of Application

1. Define the writing problem. The what of a letter of application is you
   —your work experiences, your education, your hobbies and interests.

However, what you write in such a letter is controlled by what you know about the job and by your statement of purpose. A statement of purpose is almost always the same for letters of application:

To persuade your reader to grant you an interview.

2. Make a list of those experiences you've had that your reader might value. In most cases, you can go directly to the requirements of the job and begin listing how your qualifications match those requirements.
3. Build a pattern of this information. Your first branches will eventually become the paragraphs in your letter.
4. Plan your writing: create a pre-writing plan. Follow good advertising strategy: start with your best selling point; end with your second best.
5. Write your first draft. Your introduction should include what job you are applying for and where you found out about that opening, whether it was in a newspaper or from a posting. The conclusion of your letter should ask for an interview, and should state when you are available for this interview, and how your reader can arrange the interview.

Writing Assignment 15.4

A Letter of Application

Instructions:

Find an advertisement or posting for a job you could apply for with your experience and interests. Write a letter of application for that opening.

Writing Letters of Complaint

Sometimes it's necessary to inform people about something that isn't right and what you want done about it. Perhaps a computer has charged you too much on a monthly bill, or goods you've purchased haven't lived up to their advertising. Or, perhaps a service you've been charged for hasn't been carried out properly. These and other situations call for a detailed piece of writing that first informs about the nature of your complaint and then specifies what you want changed.

Defining the writing problem is the key to writing a letter of complaint. Obviously, you know what you are writing about, but you may not know who you are writing to. And, unless you do some realistic thinking, you may not know why you are writing.

Using Your Writing Process to Write a Letter of Complaint

1. Begin to define the writing problem. Why are you writing? What do you want—just the satisfaction of complaining or do you want the computer mistake corrected, a new product to replace the defective one, or the service redone? Define the why in terms of a successful result.
2. Who is your reader? Who can do what you want done, or who can make it happen? You may need to find out the name of that person—make some phone calls. It's important that you write to the person who can do something effective. Then, think about how you can encourage that person to say *yes* to whatever you want accomplished.
3. Brainstorm. List all the information about your complaint—the sequence of events, the dates, the specifics—that your reader needs to check up on your complaint and to effect a solution.
4. Write your statement of purpose and build a pattern of your information.
5. Plan your letter. Follow what is called an inductive pattern—lead up to what you want done. Start with what is wrong and follow with what you want changed.
6. Write your first draft. Write it honestly and simply, giving the information in a straightforward manner. Your introduction should state the topic of your letter, and your conclusion should tell your reader what you want and how you want it accomplished. Any details that the reader needs to make this an easier task should be included.

Writing Assignment 15.5

A Letter of Complaint

Instructions:

Read the following case study, then write a letter of complaint to Mr. Binge.

Two weeks ago you bought a suit from the Way-Out Shop at Simples in the Endview Plaza. Simples is a national retailer with several stores in the immediate area. The store offers a pick-up and delivery service, and you have a credit account.

The first time you wore the suit, you wished you hadn't bought it. First of all, the shoulder seam ripped out. You were at a close friend's birthday party. There were more than thirty people at the party and it seemed that most of them were aware of the rip before you were. You noticed that quite a few of the guests giggled when you approached. At the same party, a button came off the jacket, and a seam in the pants unravelled to produce a small but growing hole. When you finally left the party, you were in complete disarray. Your $300 suit had fallen apart.

The next day you were angry. After a steamy coffee, you phoned Simples at Endview. The switchboard operator transferred your call to the Way-Out Shop. However, the man who took the call mumbled about being only a clerk. "Hey look, I can't do anything," he said. "Bring the suit in and show Mr. Binge. He's our department head."

You can't take the suit to the store; it's inconvenient. You have tried to telephone Mr. Binge, but he is always unavailable when you try to reach him.

You finally decide to write a letter.

References

Here are some reference books that may help you with your writing and with the preparation of your writing.

Handbooks
Bernstein, Theodore M., *The Careful Writer*. New York: Atheneum, 1972.
Brusaw, Charles T., Gerald Alred, and Walter E. Oliu, *The Business Writer's Handbook,* Second Edition. New York: St. Martin's Press, 1982.
McGraw-Hill Handbook of English, Second Canadian Edition. Toronto: McGraw-Hill Company of Canada, 1970.
Messenger, William E., and Jan de Bruyn, *The Canadian Writer's Handbook*. Toronto: Prentice-Hall Canada Inc., 1980.
Miller, Casey and Kate Swift, *The Handbook of Nonsexist Writing*. New York: Lippincott & Crowell, 1980.

Dictionaries
The Concise Oxford Dictionary. Oxford: Oxford University Press, 1982.
The Gage Canadian Dictionary. Toronto: Gage Educational Publishing, 1973.
Webster's New Collegiate Dictionary. Springfield: Thomas Allen & Son, 1977.

Spelling and Synonyms
Feinstein, George, *Programmed Spelling Demons*. Englewood Cliffs: Prentice-Hall Inc., 1973
Fergus, Patricia M., *Spelling Improvement: A Program for Self Instruction.* New York: McGraw-Hill Book Company, 1973.
Kreivsky, Joseph and Jordon L. Linfield, *Bad Spellers Dictionary*. New York: Random House, 1967.
Roget's Thesaurus in Dictionary Form. New York: G.P. Putnam's Sons, 1964.

Stoner, Oliver, ed., *The Awful Spellers Dictionary,* Revised and Anglicized Edition. London: Wolfe Publishing Ltd., 1964.

Webster's Instant Word Guide. Springfield: G & C. Merriam Company, 1980.

Résumé Preparation

Gaymer, Rosemary., *Teach Yourself How To Find a Job.* Toronto: University and College Placement Association, 1978.

Guide to Résumé Writing. Toronto: University and College Placement Association, 1978.

Answers to Selected Exercises

Exercise 2.2

The following are opinions: 1, 3, 6, 7, 9, 13, 16, 20.

Exercise 4.2

The following statements could not act as control statements: 1, 2, 4, 5, 7, 9, 10.

Possible re-writes:

1. Smoking is harmful to your health.
2. Flying hang-gliders is a dangerous hobby.
4. Hagood Hardy's "The Homecoming" is a popular piece of music.
5. Russia and the U.S. have been talking about peaceful coexistence for many years.
7. The current budget's effects are not stimulating the economy.
9. Many experts are predicting that marijuana will be legal someday.
10. Saturday afternoon at the football game is a good time.

Exercise 5.1

The following piece of information does *not* fit into the pattern:

—Millions of dollars are being spent by governments and companies to develop solar energy.

Here is one pattern of the information; yours might be very different.

Pattern for Exercise 5.1

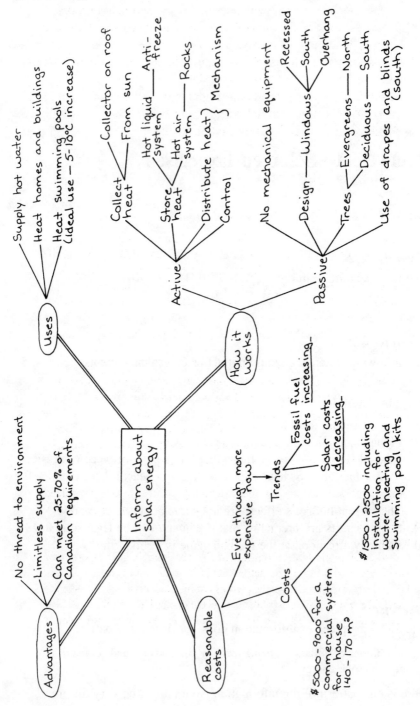

Exercise 8.1—Suggested Answers

1. *Meerschaum* is a mineral which is soft, white and heat resistant.
2. *Ophthalmology* is the branch of medicine which deals with the eye, its structure, functions and diseases.
3. *Epistemology* is a philosophical study which deals with the nature, origin, methods and limits of knowledge.
4. A *navicular* is a boat-shaped bone found in the human wrist and foot.
5. A *platypus* is a water animal with brownish fur, a duck-like bill and webbed feet, found in Australia and Tasmania.

Exercise 8.2

Each verb in the following passage is italicized:

Steve Podborski *grew* up in the suburb of Don Mills on the outskirts of Toronto. Don Mills *is* the original Canadian suburb. Its curling streets *are* the model for the cookie-cutter pattern that *has* since *been stamped* out all across the country. He first *skied* on a nearby hill about 100 feet high. But from the age of 2½ to 14, he *skied* at Collingwood, two hours by car north of Toronto, on Blue Mountain, which at 600 feet *is* a mountain in name only. World Cup downhill courses *fall* through a minimum of 3,000 vertical feet...

The terrain of the Craigleith Ski Club at Collingwood *was* nevertheless appropriate for his first introduction to the techniques of downhill skiing. He and his brother *played* a game after each day's skiing: they *would storm* straight down from the top of the hill without turning. The idea *was* to gain enough speed to cover the long, flat stretch to their parents' chalet without having to walk or pole. That *taught* him sliding, an uncoachable skill that *can earn* vital microseconds on the long, high-speed flats of the World Cup downhills.

When Podborski *was* 9 the machinery of the highly organized Southern Ontario Ski Zone *took* over. He *started* racing in the Nancy Greene League, a series of interclub tourneys for the youngest racers, unique to southern Ontario at the time. At 13 he *was competing* in the Canadian Juvenile Championships in British Columbia. By 16 he *had earned* an invitation to the national team's annual fall selection camp. He *was expected* to admire the prowess of his elders but not to make the team. There *were* five downhills held at the camp. He *won* them all. "It *was* phenomenal," he *recalls*. "I *couldn't believe* it. Neither *could* they." He *made* the team.

Exercise 8.3

Here are the subject/verb combinations in the passage:

Subject	Verb
Steve Podborski	grew
Don Mills	is
streets	are
that	has been stamped
he	skied
he	skied
which	is
downhill courses	fall
terrain	was
He and his brother	played
they	would storm
idea	was
that	taught
that	can earn
Podborski	was
machinery	took
He	started
he	was competing
he	had earned
He	was expected
five downhills	were
He	won
It	was
he	recalls
I	couldn't believe
they	could
He	made

Exercise 8.4

Each fragment in the paragraph is underlined. Make sure your re-write has fixed these mistakes.

People in southern Ontario get very excited about snow-storms. They will tell you, for instance, about the "Blizzard of '78." How it was one of the worst storms in history. On January 26, the storm with howling winds that were recorded at over 170 km/h. Even though the radio stations had been warning drivers about the storm. Many drivers were caught unprepared. Were stranded on the roads all over the province. In one Service Center which is located on the MacDonald-Cartier Freeway west of London. Three hundred motorists were trapped for two days and a night. Others stayed in their cars. People who owned snowmobiles and four-wheel-drive trucks. Struggling through 3 m high snowdrifts, pushing stranded cars, rescuing motorists. In homes across the province, members of families waited. Some homes lost electricity and heat. In some communities, the hydro lines blown down in the 120 km/h winds. Before everything finally returned to a normal winter situation. Millions of dollars in property damage and many lives.

In the west, people don't become quite so hysterical about a little snowstorm.

Exercise 8.5—Suggested Answers

Questions 5 and 7 are correct.

1. Your sales are up; therefore, your bonus is forthcoming.
2. We sent your order #7320 to the Saskatoon store. The bill of lading is enclosed.
3. Her work is still inferior; nevertheless, she is improving.
4. This report analyzes our new fast foods division. It makes three recommendations.
5. While she was in Montréal, her secretary handled her correspondence.
6. The advertising campaign, launched on December 1, has had startling effects. Sales are up 73% over last year.
7. I have consulted the legal division and am waiting for a decision.
8. The proposal was submitted on January 5. Then I waited for a decision.
9. The meeting was postponed. No alternative date was set.
10. Your order for 15 gross of #27 fasteners arrived today; however, we are unsure about your shipping instructions.

Exercise 9.1

In the sentences below, each focus is boxed, and each emphasis is underlined.

1. Mary got home at 5:00 p.m.
2. Because he had to work late, Murray didn't get home until 7:00 p.m.

3. The ball game was over and the players were tired.

4. When the match was over, the team was exhausted.

5. Bill and his mother went to the movie.

6. As Eric couldn't go to the movie, his mother and sister went without him.

7. After the road went through the village, Moffat became much noisier and a place where no one wanted to live.

8. The policemen questioned the people who saw the accident.

9. Jim worked and saved his money, but when the price of the sports car was increased, he couldn't buy it.

10. Although the company faced a year that was predicted to be economically bad, the managers installed a computer.

Exercise 9.2—Possible Re-writes

1. Finding a good chocolate bar isn't easy.
2. Because the test was on last term's work, it fooled me completely.
3. OK as it is.
4. The low-scoring football game was dull.
5. Anna broke off her engagement with John on the weekend. She doesn't seem to want to marry him.
6. November is a long month and the fact that there are no holidays makes it seem even longer.
7. Fred went to work for his father. His remaining unemployed seemed ridiculous.
8. Scott asked if I had lied to him. This question angered me.
9. Gina's brilliance is apparent.
10. He took the job that pays the most money. This action shouldn't surprise you.

Exercise 9.3—Possible Re-writes

1. As dawn breaks, the pine trees darken against the sky.
2. Tiny toy soldiers carved from black walnut are in the basket.
3. An old potbellied stove sits just inside the door.
4. The smell of onion and garlic spaghetti sauce hits you right at the doorway.

5. The fastest, most complete conveyer system in North America is in our new factory.
6. The closing bell sounds at four o'clock. Hurrying children soon fill the school yard.
7. Expensive paintings hang on their living room walls.
8. Down the stream, the fallen trees sink into the water.
9. The foreman has paid little attention to the order of the merchandise.
10. OK as it is, or this:
    Niagara Falls is visible from the observation deck of the CN Tower.

Exercise 10.1

1. Noun clause
2. Adjective clause
3. Adjective phrase—prepositional
4. Adjectives
5. Gerund phrase
6. Present participle phrase—adjective
7. Appositive
8. Adverb clause
9. Adverb
10. Infinitive phrase—noun
11. Past participle phrase—adjective
12. Adverb phrase—prepositional
13. Adverb
14. Adjective clause
15. Infinitive phrase—adverb

Exercise 10.2—Possible Re-writes

1. Jim saw the dog running with his tail between his legs.
2. He arrived at the new airport, the biggest facility in the world.
3. Mary took Bob, who was dressed in a rented tuxedo, to the formal.
4. He did excellently on his exams.
5. During the evening, he drank almost fifteen cups of coffee.
6. Loaded down with extra equipment, our new car arrived at the dealership.
7. Everyone enjoys pancakes when they are served with butter and maple syrup.
8. Before we stopped for a rest, the bench looked inviting.

9. The company is sending the package tomorow.
10. This recipe can be prepared in twenty minutes.
11. He was moderately skilled in fishing.
12. While they were waiting in line for the concert tickets, the rain stopped.
13. After watching the sunset, I felt like taking a walk.
14. The Festival of Friends, which is the largest outside free music event in Canada, is held annually in Hamilton.
15. For a day, they thought about taking a trip around the world, but they chose not to.
16. Ellen watched the thunderstorm while she was doing her homework.
17. In November, everyone in Canada is in a bad mood.
18. They carried her home, drunk.
19. The car circled the house and then disappeared.
20. He is reliable.

Exercise 10.3—Possible Re-writes

1. To serve and to protect are the policeman's responsibilities.
2. The house with the indoor swimming pool and the view of the Pacific Ocean is for sale.
3. A sporting goods company has just announced the development of an indestructible and inexpensive hockey stick.
4. Situated in the middle of the room and covered with a throwrug sits a white corduroy couch.
5. The house was sold quickly and easily.
6. He found the treasure either by deducing the route to the cache or by torturing the only man who knew the location.
7. OK
8. If the book is not published, the decision was made either because the story is unsaleable or because the author is unknown.
9. She dreams of neither having material goods nor being a famous person.
10. The room was not only large, but also unfurnished.

Exercise 11.1—Possible Re-writes

1. Susan *has forgotten* the date of her graduation.
2. Last night at Leslie's party, Eva *ignored* me.
3. His speech *rambled*.

4. He left school because he was broke.
5. He *tiptoed* towards the door.
6. Stephen *distrusted* his partner.
7. Sharon *received* the new scholarship.
8. The two lovers *whispered* in the corner of the café.
9. Ernie *slouched*.
10. At the meeting, Catherine *reported* on the conditions on the reserve.

Exercise 11.2 — Possible Re-writes

1. Many students take part-time jobs.
2. Someone blew out all the candles on the cake.
3. Matthew redesigned the filing system.
4. OK
5. Mrs. Grady is editing the new book.
6. Parliament defeated the private member's bill.
7. OK
8. Because of the mail strike, a courier is delivering the contract.
9. By the time I got to the store, shoppers had bought all the specials.
10. Wayne Gretzky set the scoring record.

Exercise 11.3 — Possible Re-writes

1. Fifteen minutes before closing time, that employee *sneaks* away from the factory.
2. Squirrels *scamper* over the attic floor.
3. The boys *play* in Mr. Glasgow's orchard.
4. Huge bonfires *smoulder* in the distant fields.
5. They were extremely tired, and began to *despair*.
6. Off in the distance, apartment buildings rise from the horizon.
7. OK
8. The armies are battling on the plains.
9. By the time I get to Kingston, she will miss me.
10. The exhaust from the buses *fills* the closed terminal.

Exercise 11.4 — Possible Re-writes

1. Little time remains.
2. A storm approaches from the west.

3. Three men were trapped in the warehouse when it burned.
4. An old typewriter needing repairs sits up in the attic.
5. Mr. Jones' estate has good soil, but on Bill Smith's farm weeds grow in the swamps and around the boulders.
6. Seven turrets surround the old castle.
7. A tremendous spirit inspires that team.
8. If the food supply is not increased, great despair will spread throughout the world.
9. Only one man can solve that problem.
10. The old and the new blend in their home.

Exercise 11.5 — Possible Re-writes

1. The CN Tower *dwarfs* all the other buildings in Toronto.
2. Three mighty pine trees *shield* the house from the road.
3. Research indicates that people *hitchhike* a little more cautiously now than a few years ago.
4. The red couch *brightens* the dull living room.
5. OK
6. That magazine *reports* the news as well as any other.
7. The sportscaster *presents* local sports stories at 6:40 p.m.
8. Your three cousins *are coming* to the party.
9. Those books *shot* up the best seller list.
10. OK

Exercise 12.1

Here are the passages with the verbs corrected.

Diary Entry

I am in Montréal, stay~~ed~~ *ing* at Place Bonaventure. My room face~~d~~ *s* the Place Ville-Marie. Below me in the evening lights, I ~~saw~~ *see* the people moving across the patios. Some ~~were~~ *are* in a hurry, others walk leisurely. I ~~couldn't~~ *can't* distinguish anything else as my room is on the seventeenth floor and it ~~was~~ *is* even difficult to make out the sex of the pedestrians. The sun set quickly this evening. I watch *ed* it during my vigil. I watched it

moving down to the tall buildings and the mountains that
~~were~~ *are* in the west. Then it disappeared, as if some monster ~~will~~ *had*
~~eat~~ *eaten* it with a greedy gulp.

Our new house will be ready in three months. Right now, the
foundations ~~were~~ *are* complete. It ~~didn't~~ *doesn't* look like the house of our
dreams as it sits in the mud and rubble that construction sites
~~will~~ create. But we are enthusiastic. We ~~could~~ *can* see the skeleton
of our dream house. Yesterday we walked over the site with the
architect's drawings. We use*d* our imaginations. We ~~see~~ *saw* the
living room furnished and hear*d* the children playing in the
family room downstairs. We *will* have a magnificent house.

Exercise 12.2

The incorrect verb forms have been corrected:

1. The new speedboat has ~~ran~~ *run* into a snag.
2. The frozen water pipe had ~~blew~~ *blown* apart the night before.
3. I had ~~laid~~ *lain* down for a rest just before she arrived.
4. I had ~~rode~~ *ridden* around before I met him.
5. I'm sure I ~~lay~~ *laid* the book on that shelf.
6. He told me that I'd better ~~set~~ *sit* down before he ~~gives~~ *gave* me the news.
7. She had ~~mistook~~ *mistaken* the girl for an old friend.
8. I have ~~swam~~ *swum* over a mile.
9. The temperature has ~~rose~~ *risen* over the last hour.
10. The trapper ~~hanged~~ *hung* the wolf carcass from a tree.

Exercise 12.3

1. My interest in sports *goes* back to my childhood.
2. November or February *is* the best time to go south.

3. They *have* drunk too much.
4. There *were* a few sale items left.
5. The size and price of the book *have* been increased.
6. The builders or the architect *plans* to see you in the morning.
7. Where *are* the nails and the hammer?
8. Mary, as well as her sister, *attends* this school.
9. The seven books and the notebook *belong* to my sister.
10. Each of the men *is* talented.
11. *Is* there one or two *N*'s in her name?
12. She is one of those people who *believe* in nuclear disarmament.
13. The realization of fame and fortune *causes* problems for some people.
14. The desk with its ornate brassware and unusual accessories *is* for sale.
15. A flock of geese *is* flying over my house.

Exercise 13.1

1. Jan and Lori met to discuss the failure of ~~her~~ *Jan's* business.
2. Bill's father is a scientist, but Bill is not interested in ~~it~~ *science*.
3. Fourteen cars piled up on the Trans-Canada Highway, but ~~it~~ *the accident* did not hurt anyone.
4. ~~Everyone~~ *all the people* at the party enjoyed themselves.
5. The teacher accused ~~we~~ *us* students of being impolite.
6. Everyone except Roger and ~~I~~ *me* was on time for the game..
7. Sheila is as tall as ~~me~~ *I*.
8. Students writing tests often become very nervous. Therefore I think ~~they~~ *tests* should be abolished.
9. The trapper charged a lot of money for the ermine's skin because ~~they~~ *ermines* are hard to catch.
10. ~~Each of~~ the plumbers cast ~~his~~ *their* ballot*s* for the new contract.

Exercise 14.1

1. Your order of belt buckles *was* shipped yesterday.
   (subject/verb agreement)
2. Your sales representative told us to send it to Kamloops; however,

the order specified it should be sent to Red Deer.
(run-on sentence)

3. Our representative visited your area last week.
(verb tense)

4. He told Mr. Smith that Mr. Smith's proposal had been turned down.
(pronoun reference)

5. That proposal was an interesting one. He promised to give jobs to everyone, to lower the cost of living and to increase the profits of local businesses.
(parallelism)

6. The seminar which has an agenda posted on the bulletin board is scheduled in the conference room.
(misplaced subordination)

7. The schedule of events may change.
(fragment)

8. All taxpayers receive the booklet they need to complete their returns.
(pronoun gender)

9. Using the booklet, you can complete your tax return easily.
(dangling subordination)

10. The accuracy of the returns has improved noticeably.
(adjective/adverb)

Exercise 14.2

The first thing you should check when you ~~by~~ *buy* a puppy is the temper*a*ment of the dog. One principa*le* I have found sound is to*o* check the sire or dam*e*. If they are fr*ei*ndly, then the puppy will probably be ~~alright~~ *all right*. Another thing you should examine is the bone structure. Put the dog in a station*a*ry po*i*sition and feel him; make sure the hips are not l*o*se. This check is e*s*pecia*l*ly important because of the risk of hip dis*l*acia.

You should definit*e*ly consider ~~you're facityo~~ *your facilities*. Don't forget that that cute little puppy will grow up and might not be so cute. This advi*c*e is good because some dogs have to have a great deal of exercise and some big dogs*,* such as St. Bern*a*rds

or Great Danes cost a small fortune to feed. Finally, the fo*u*rth
point is that you should have the puppy checked by a
veter*i*narian. This coun*sel* could save you money and aggrava-
*t*ion. Of co*u*rse, no vet can prophe*s*y ~~weather~~ *whether* or not a little
puppy will be a long-living, healthy dog, but he *or she* can check for
puppy problems. Let the vet *a*ffect your decision. Don't throw
away mon*e*y just bec*au*se you feel sorry for a cute little puppy.

Index